W9-BAC-064

. 88/08

THE SOVIET STATE:
AN AGING REVOLUTION

Other books by the author:

SOVIET COMMUNES
THE AMERICAN PROBLEM
THE IMPERIAL ORDER
SOVIET FOREIGN POLICY IN PERSPECTIVE
THE SOVIET RUSSIAN STATE

THE SOVIET STATE:
AN AGING REVOLUTION

Robert G. Wesson
University of California
Santa Barbara

JOHN WILEY & SONS, INC.

New York   London   Sydney   Toronto

Copyright © 1972, by John Wiley & Sons. Inc.

All rights reserved. Published simultaneously in Canada.

No part of this book may be reproduced by any means, nor
transmitted, nor translated into a machine language without the written permission of the publisher.

Library of Congress Cataloging in Publication Data

Wesson, Robert G
    The Soviet state, an aging revolution.

    1.   Russia—Politics and government—1917-
I.   Title.
JN6515. 1972.W472   320.9′47′084   72-000032
ISBN 0-471-93375-9

Printed in the United States of America

10 9 8 7 6 5 4 3 2 1

PREFACE

The Soviet Union is not only the other superpower, holder of enormous power and wielder of great influence. It also represents the principal political alternative to the liberal-capitalistic-pluralistic society prevalent in the Western world. The two biggest signposts to the future are the Western-American and the Soviet-Russian, standing for the looser-individualistic and the more organized collectivistic. Of these, the latter has seemed notably successful in recent decades. Not only have Soviet power and influence grown tremendously from the feeble beginnings of half a century ago; Soviet doctrines and institutions have served as basic inspiration for radicals everywhere even those who have turned their backs on the Soviet state like the Maoists. The innumerable one-party regimes in the world owe much to Lenin, who inaugurated the form of revolutionary-modernizing-authoritarian state. The intellectual importance of Marxism likewise owes much to its success as the official ideology of the Soviet state and many imitators. Without accepting the Marxist-Leninist vision of history, we can agree that the Bolshevik seizure of power and the establishment of the new Soviet state was probably the most important planned political event of all time and truly ushered in a new era.

Despite this, or because of it, understanding of the Soviet system is difficult. There is no agreement among scholars on evaluation or approach or even, in many cases, on important facts. This is partly because political science is inevitably involved in politics and few issues are more emotional than those relating to the Soviet Union and its challenge to traditional ways. It is partly because the Russians are unhelpful. Those responsible for guiding the Soviet press do not seek to enlighten regarding the innersprings of politics and decision-making; it was some-what sensational when Brezhnev recently revealed that the Politburo met weekly. Soviet media are to inspire and educate, not to analyze political issues, and the analyst draws conclusions from them at his risk. Yet our understanding of Soviet affairs is inevitably based almost en-tirely on Soviet sources feebly supplemented by personal observations and, in the last few years, by the growing unauthorized press, col-lectively known as "Samizdat." A further difficulty is that words are used differently in Soviet and Western contexts. The idea of freely com-peting political parties is strange to the Russians; "party" for them means not an organization contending for political advantage but the group governing the country in the name of Marxism-Leninism and the workers. "Democracy" means a certain deference to forms of popular sovereignty, equalitarianism, maximum public participation in the exe-cution of programs and the idea that the party expresses the will and fills the needs of the masses. As Soviet writers make clear, it does not imply contested elections or freedom of political agitation. Many other terms of the Western political lexicon similarly carry different signifi-cance when adapted to the Soviet scene.

All approaches to Soviet politics suffer severe limitations both in methodology and shortage of data. The analysis here presented is primarily historical-functional, emphasizing the continuity of the Rus-sian-Soviet experience and the functions served by ideology and insti-tutions. The Soviet state is perhaps more than most the product of its dramatic past; yet the Soviet political structure has largely been de-signed for definite and understandable purposes. Implicit in this ap-proach is also the conviction that human psychology and the essentials of politics are much alike whether the state calls itself "socialist" or "liberal." Historical stress does not deny but rather implies that the Soviet state has changed and will continue to change; it is the author's conviction that it must be much altered within a decade or so. Implicit in any consideration of the Soviet government is comparison with the American. Hence differences receive more attention than resemblances. The latter may become equally important; it is perhaps essential that they do so if the two systems are to survive together on this small planet.

This work seeks to draw no moral conclusions, only to present fairly the realities. It can be realistically recognized that pluralism and diversity are much less in the Soviet Union than in Western societies, hence that freedom as usually understood is less in the former. It is a matter of individual preference if one assesses more highly discipline and centrally directed purposefulness or a perhaps anarchic liberty. Soviet vices and virtues are different from those of the "bourgeois" West, and the virtues may be other than those claimed. The Soviet system, being different, should be recognized as uncongenial to many Western values; this does not mean that it does not have values of its own.

This book is based on *The Soviet Russian State,* recently published by John Wiley and Sons, Inc., abbreviated to make it accessible to a larger audience. For bibliography and citations as well as fuller development of the argument the reader is referred to the larger work. The sources of this work are those of *The Soviet Russian State,* and the acknowledgments made there are valid here. Special thanks are owed to Professor Robert Casier for his helpful suggestions.

Santa Barbara, California   *Robert G. Wesson*

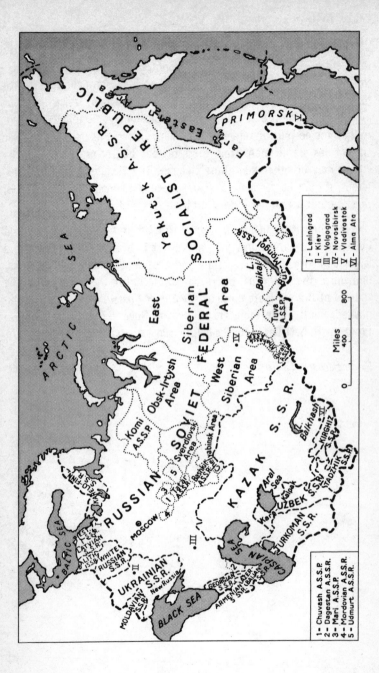

CONTENTS

INTRODUCTION

What the Soviet Union is Like

In various ways the United States and the Soviet Union are much alike. Their populations are similar (the Soviet being a fifth larger), and they are the only industrialized nations in the top population bracket. Both are dominantly of European racial stock and have modified Europe-based cultures. They are among the largest countries of the earth, and if the Soviet Union is two and a half times the United States in area this may be discounted in view of its large arctic and subarctic wasteland. Correspondingly, they show much diversity within their vastness, and both face major problems of integration or adjustment, of races in the United States, of nationalities in the Soviet Union. By virtue of size and development, they are the only two powers with major strategic military strength and the only two in a position to play really global roles. In total economic weight they are in the same class, although Soviet wealth lags well behind American. There is something similar in Soviet and American characters, too, as both

1

have a certain dash and exuberance, a heartiness and fondness for bigness. Both have had confidence in their ability to remake the world.

Yet the United States and the Soviet Union have usually regarded one another as political opposites, each representing for the other practically the center of evil in the world. The political contrast was strongest twenty years ago when the land of the Soviets, under the grim rule of Joseph Stalin, was practically a closed kingdom, permitting only the necessary minimum of agents to travel abroad and admitting only a few persons with official business and a handful of journalists. Life was austere within the fortress, as Russians were driven to produce ever more but received little in return. Fear was everywhere, and conformity was outwardly absolute.

Much has changed. Many thousand Soviet citizens go to foreign countries, and hundreds of thousands of tourists visit the Soviet Union, not only from satellite countries but from the Western world. Among them are fifty thousand or so Americans yearly, only a tiny fraction of the numbers touring such small lands as the Netherlands or Ireland but enough that travel to Russia is considered commonplace. Russians are still unlikely to invite foreigners to visit their homes, but they are not much afraid to be seen talking with them and may well venture some critical opinions. At the same time life has materially brightened. Soviet faces have taken on more cheerful looks, and the foreigner no longer stands out by virtue of being smartly dressed. The shop windows of Gorky street, Moscow's main thoroughfare, are bright and filled with attractive wares. Fashion-conscious Soviet girls use abundant makeup, Muscovites line up for rides on a ferris wheel, and the once solemnly empty boulevards of Moscow are jammed with rush hour traffic.

But the ordering of Soviet society remains different. This immediately strikes the tourist who learns that he can see the sights of Moscow only as the guest of a state agency, Intourist. He goes to Western Europe without a visa and makes whatever arrangements he sees fit; for the Soviet Union, he makes arrangements in advance for a fixed itinerary and a certain number of days. He does not wander according to fancy; although many cities have been opened, the bulk of the land, including nearly all Siberia, is off limits. On looking around, the Western tourist in the Soviet Union finds more than onion-topped old churches to remind him that he is far from home. If he reads Russian, he sees a great deal of political but almost no commercial advertising. He finds no non-Communist newspapers, unless perhaps under the counter of one of the main tourist hotels. The Soviet kiosk offers little to correspond to what he has been accustomed to, no sexy magazines or books, practically nothing frivolous, but a mass of political or semipolitical and technical writing. Any Soviet paper—they are all much alike—makes a marked contrast with such papers as the *Los Angeles Times.* The Soviet news-sheet fills most of its four pages with serious material, mostly information and exhortation for increased production, with stories designed for political inspiration. Its photographs are of factories, outstanding workers and dedicated soldiers, occasionally of approved political leaders. Television programs are usually edifying, never naughty, and unburdened by commercials, unless exhortations to support the party may be so considered. Most striking is the uniformity of media; not only all papers but also books, radio, television and the cinema pound out a single great message, with differences usually imperceptible except to the attentive student.

Uniformity summarizes much of the specialness of Soviet life as seen from the Western point of view. In cities like Moscow and Leningrad, not to speak of outlying regions like Central Asia there is substantial diversity of architecture; but this is only because buildings are permanent, and the constructions of pre-Soviet days mingle with Stalinist-ornate and modern massive-functional. The building going on from Vladivostok to Brest-Litovsk (and beyond, in Eastern Europe) is all almost of a single style. In similar fashion, Soviet enterprises, manufacturing plants, offices, stores, and the like have in common their usually severe styles. This is hardly surprising as they all belong, practically speaking, to one giant firm, the Soviet state. If the tourist is able to investigate, he will likewise find that all governmental divisions, from the village to the Union government, are managed in the same manner, all being parts of a single huge apparatus.

If this is a curiosity for the visitor, it is the stuff of life for the Soviet citizen. His existence in many ways is not unlike that of the American: he goes daily to work in office or factory—probably not working quite so hard—rests and plays, is apt to get drunk more often, and certainly takes more pride in taking his vodka straight. He, or at least his children, likes modern music; and when his marriage sours he gets divorced at about the same rate as Americans. But in many other ways the Soviet world is almost opposite from the American. There is an almost total absence of public political, social, or economic controversy; the mental atmosphere is troubled neither by conflicts of political philosophy nor such issues as women's liberation, the supersonic transport, and dangers from nuclear radiation. In a noncompetitive economy, the Soviet citizen is rather secure, with little fear of failure to find a job according to his qualifications upon graduation (the state trains the specialists it expects to need) or of being jobless thereafter. He has little need to save money. Indeed, he has little use for savings—no securities, land investments, etc., only savings accounts and the state lottery. His finances are simple; he does not burden himself with debt, as there are no charge accounts, and installment sales are rigidly geared to his pay. Nor can he pay by check; only official enterprises have checking accounts. He has little worry about taxes. Direct taxes are very low, as the state takes its cut through the prices of goods, which are very high in terms of his pay. In sickness he can count on medical care at state expense. The Soviet citizen also feels safer than the American in the streets at night, though it is hard to say how much this is due to a lower crime rate and how much to the lack of publicity for crime.

Life is simpler in many ways for the Soviet man. Marxism-Leninism is given to him as an answer to all questions of past and present, and no competing creeds confuse him. In all respects, he faces fewer needs to choose. One political party claims his allegiance, and at elections there is no need to vote against anyone. He hardly selects a place to live; his apartment (for which rent is nominal) probably goes with his job and is of quality reflecting his standing. Time and place of his vacation are set by the boss or trade union. School children have no choice of schools and practically none of subject. A university student picks out his institution and specialty but otherwise follows a fixed course. Similarly, the most striking difference between an American and a Soviet supermarket is not in prices or perhaps quality but in variety of goods.

In a sense, life in the Soviet Union is more coherent. Man is much more a member of a collective or community, large and small, than in the free-wheeling and incoherent Western society. There is more mutual responsibility of people, more intimacy, some would say more spirituality among Russians. One need not seek individual purpose; the grand collective purpose of the building of a superior social order is presented as absolute and undeniable. If one feels a creative urge he must strike out on no unhappy individualistic bent but must think always of the social purpose defined by the community as incorporated in the political leadership. The framework of life is far firmer than in less directed societies; to get ahead, one must conform strictly to the given order, which rewards those who adapt themselves and contribute properly and offers only hardship to rebels.

This also means that life is shaped far more by a single organized will than in less ordered lands. In other words, the Soviet universe is more politicized. Success is measured not by wealth but by political position; the important form of wealth, so to speak, is status, primarily in the hierarchy of the party. The average citizen is far more propagandized, appealed to for patriotic-socialist-internationalist sentiments, and mobilized by political authorities. His factory or workshop struggles to fulfill its share of a plan adopted by the highest powers. In spare time he is invited to work with sundry officially sponsored groups; there are practically no private organizations. All except some more or less tolerated churches are theoretically tied together in the great collectivity, with its higher social-political purpose. The aphorism of private plenty and public squalor sometimes applied to the United States is reversed in Russia. Services appropriately managed by the government are relatively good, like public transportation, public medicine, and education. Those better handled by private enterprise, such as the furnishing of goods and nonessential services, are weak.

It is consequently of supreme importance what kind of political leadership the country has. This determines if more resources are to be put into the production of consumer goods or into the continued buildup of heavy and defense industry, or whether censorship will be relaxed to permit more interesting, if less moralizing, literature. Most of all, the older generation recalls how a certain political leadership could in the past cast a pall of terror over everyone, high and low. But paradoxically the Soviet citizen of today is not interested in the higher politics; government is a sphere apart, about which he is neither consulted nor informed. People high up and far away make the decisions.

With relative security and freedom from responsibility, with deep satisfaction in the role of Russia in the world, ordinary Soviet citizens may be quite as happy as their Western counterparts, if one could compare such things. At least, those who are not troubled by a restless intelligence, those who can feel satisfied with the official answers, may well find their existences simpler and more purposeful, although probably less exciting, than they would in more hectic and disorderly societies. Even Soviet intellectuals who defect or are otherwise cast into the turbulence of Western societies find it profoundly difficult to adjust.

In brief, by politically determined circumstances, Soviet man lives in another psychological milieu from most people of the advanced industrial world. He has different problems, different satisfactions, and a different outlook even aside from the official philosophy which sets his universe apart. To cross from Helsinki to Leningrad—or from West to East Berlin—is to go from one way of life to another.

This has been true for many years. The thaw of Khrushchev days and his partial opening to the West were more promise than deep change, and they have been turned back. Earlier, in the middle 1920's, there was much stronger evidence that the gulf between Russia and the West was narrowing, yet in a few years the excesses of Stalinism followed. It was the meaning of Lenin's revolution in 1917 to set Russia in opposition to the West, so far as it declined to follow the Russian lead.

Yet the distinctness of Russia antedates the Bolshevik Revolution, which could not have happened in a Western country. Russia before the First World War was an alien and somewhat mysterious universe for Frenchmen and Britons. Even as Russia under the last tsar was becoming more westernized than before or after, it seemed part-Oriental in outlook and politics. Hence, to begin the study of Soviet Russia as a separate political genus, it is well to delve far into the past, in hopes of finding some clues to the Soviet system. Lenin and his fellows claimed they were building a wholly new political structure, but they had to use the materials of the old Russia and to build on its foundations.

PART ONE

HOW
THE SOVIET SYSTEM
CAME ABOUT

CHAPTER 1

Historic Continuity

IMPERIAL UNIVERSALISM

"Scratch a Russian and find a Tatar," the old saying ran. The alienness of Russia from the Western world goes back to its conquest by Tatars (or Mongols) in the thirteenth century and the new Russian state which arose within Tatar hegemony in the fifteenth century. Previously Kievan Russia of the eleventh and twelfth centuries was a collection of small principalities and trading towns not greatly different from those rising all over Europe. But warriors flooding over the steppes from the faraway Mongolian plains held nearly all the Russian lands in thrall for some two centuries. Coming out from under the Mongol yoke, Russia found itself handicapped by a technical-cultural lag which, despite some spurts, it has never been able fully to overcome and which has made Russian relations with the West chronically difficult. Russia was also divorced from Western political tradition, as it took practical lessons in authoritarianism from the Tatars. They taught their Russian subjects the arts of tax-gathering, census-taking, conscription, and postal communication. They introduced the death penalty, judicial torture, and the concept of the sovereign as owner of the state and master of all. They furnished the model of a huge, absolutist, and effectively taxed empire unlike anything in Western Europe since the Roman empire.

8

The Mongols also opened the way to indefinite expansion of Russia across Asia, as the decay of their enormous empire left a corresponding area of weakness. Rising at first by service to the Khans, the prince of Moscow gathered larger and larger territories under his own aegis until he could cast off the Mongol hegemony and unite the Russian lands in a campaign of liberation against these alien and heathen forces, sometimes called the Golden Horde. About the time Muscovy was shaking off alien domination, the Byzantine empire was finally liquidated by the Turks. The rulers of Russia now regarded themselves as the upholders of the Orthodox faith in the world, successors of the Caesars of Byzantium and of Rome, who had claimed rightful dominion of the universe. Liberation merged into conquest; the unification of Russia was inseparable from rapid expansion into alien lands. Idealized as heir to the Byzantine empire, Russia became in fact heir of the Mongol khans.

The Russian empire, taking shape in the latter part of the fifteenth century, went forward for many generations, mostly by slow pressure, sometimes halting but rarely retreating. Like the overseas empires of Western European states—Portugal, Spain, Holland, etc.—being formed concurrently, it was made possible by technological superiority. Russia was close enough to the West, geographically and culturally, to borrow readily the instruments of warfare and rulership, while most of its neighbors remained more backward; it was the only semi-European power with a backyard stretching indefinitely in Asia.

The growth of the Russian empire was at first simply a continuation of the conflict with the Mongols, which knew no stopping point on the endless plains. It was a crusade of Russian Orthodox Christianity against heathens or heretics on the frontiers. It was a civilizing mission. Everywhere the Russians strode forth as bearers of justice, peace, and righteousness, protectors of all peoples. Their overriding purpose was to build strength; expansion meant greatness and security. Empire was the glory of the rulers and made Russia invincible against the ever-present threat of a technologically superior West. Unlike the overseas empires, it was contiguous; the few noncontiguous acquisitions, like Alaska, were readily relinquished. The new lands were not held as colonies but were incorporated into the Russian state, becoming integral and inseparable parts of the sacred body of the empire.

Russia thus became a multinational continental empire, a polity very different from the nation-states of the West. As early as the sixteenth century, it had engulfed not only a multitude of small Russian states but large numbers of Finns and Tatars; to them were added Ukrainians, Turkic peoples of Central Asia, the great and small nationalities of the Caucasus, Balts, Poles, and many others. In the medley of races and cultures, cemented by force, bureaucracy, loyalty to the tsar, and to some extent orthodoxy, the Russian core comprised much less than half of the total.

This composite state so much grander than ordinary nations was—and is—extremely impressive. As Gogol wrote, "What does this limitless space prophesy? Is not limitless thought to be born here, when thou art limitless? Is not here a land for the great. . . ?" "One has but to look at a map of the world to be filled with holy awe at the future destinies of Russia," wrote a Russian publicist in 1831. It was natural that Russia should dream of mastery of the globe, which seemed its appointed destiny. In the infancy of the empire, pious Russians regarded their tsar as more than an ordinary monarch; at the end of the fifteenth century, a monk wrote to Ivan III, "All kingdoms of the Orthodox Christian faith are merged into thy kingdom. Thou alone, in all that is under heaven, art a Christian tsar . . . two Romes have fallen, but the Third stands, and there will be no fourth."[1] Russia should be the center of the believing world. Belief that Russia, or the Russian ideal, should rule indefinitely continued through the nineteenth century, finding eloquent expression in such writers as Danilevsky and Dostoievsky. The latter saw the Russians as a peculiarly universal people, called upon to overcome the divisions of mankind by the "all-uniting Russian soul."

There was in this no sense of aggressiveness but enormous self-righteousness. Danilevsky, eager for territorial and cultural expansion, found Russia uniquely free from greed for power; and Dostoievsky saw the empire based on the thirst for brotherly unity. In conquering and civilizing, the Russians felt themselves to be fulfilling a noble duty for peace, unity, and the redemption of mankind. Radicals opposed to tsarist government were hardly less imbued with the vocation of the Russian people to lead the brotherhood of humanity.

AUTOCRACY

Immensity made autocracy inevitable. The huge realm elevated the rulership as the symbol of unity and submerged the individual. It called for firm control to secure the coherence of the whole. There was no room in the imperial scheme for autonomous rights of any province or group; no division should blemish its exalted unity. The tsar claimed, and his subjects believed, that the defense of the realm and its integrity required a single unquestioned authority with total command of the instruments of force. The principle of the Russian world, from the fifteenth century to the present, has been union, in antithesis to the divisiveness—anarchy, as it has seemed to Russians—of the West.

Ivan III, who first greatly expanded the Muscovite state, set himself up formally as autocrat. Ivan IV (the Terrible), who also greatly enlarged Russian dominions, regarded all his subjects, high and low, as his slaves and executed many of the old nobility who were insufficiently humble. Peter the Great, who went to great lengths to modernize and westernize his land, terrorized all, hardened the enserfment of the peasants and the obligations of the gentry, and proclaimed his absolutism juridically. Despite infiltration of Western ideas in the following two centuries, the tsar's autocratic power continued to be upheld as indispensable. Although admittedly mortal in body, he was divine in authority; and the realm in theory was his estate. Defeats, first in the Crimean War (1854) and then in the war against Japan (1904), led to some relaxation of absolutism, and the half-revolution of 1905 forced the tsar to concede a half-constitution. But this never amounted to more than a veneer, and the last tsar, Nicholas II, staunchly upheld the principle of his unrestricted authority.

The tsar was Father of his Country, to whom all his children owed unquestioning and reverent submission. The adjective "holy" was freely applied both to Russia and to its ruler; subjects eager to please Peter the Great equated him with God. It was the tsar who conferred all authority. There were no real institutions apart from his office, only instruments and extensions of it. Justice and legality had meaning only in relation to his sovereign will.

So far as there was pressure for a constitution, it was because of Western influences and examples. Russia was too big for a national assembly to be practical, and the tsar had no need to secure the concurrence of a burgher class for his taxes. In the nineteenth century, various tsars mulled over constitutional schemes which would have supposedly broadened participation in the government and so given it a sounder basis without appreciably restricting the will of the autocrat. Nothing came of such schemes; and true conservatives remained convinced that a constitution would be the ruin of Russia, even as liberals began demanding constitutional government as essential to catching up with the West.

In the absence of a constitution, there was little legal order. Right conduct was the loyal carrying out of the sovereign will, not conformity to legality. The administrators and the military held the empire together and formed the ruling classes. Promotion was theoretically by merit but usually by seniority or favor; it became more dependent on intrigue as one approached the summit, where cliques competed for the ear of the tsar. Russian literature abounds in satires on the ignorance, indolence, and venality of lower officials; but the apparatus managed to fulfill its necessary functions.

Despite its immensity and diversity, the state was highly centralized and left minimal scope for any kind of local autonomy. It was feared that any concessions to local separatism would only raise demands for more. In imitation of Western institutions, Catherine II established self-governing bodies of cities and of local nobility, but they were endowed with no real powers and became lifeless organs of administration.

A large police force, regular and political, was necessary; and there were manifold although ordinarily ineffective controls over all potentially dangerous activities. Unauthorized associations, theoretically even informal discussion groups, were banned by law. By the passport system (which was anathema to revolutionaries, including Lenin, but which Stalin reinstated) everyone needed a passport to travel away from his place of residence. Travellers had to register with police, and a permit was required for a change of residence. Police agents were everywhere. At a time when international movement in most of Europe was very casual, Russia had strict controls of exit and entry. Although bars were somewhat lowered after 1860, it was long difficult for nonofficial Russians to leave their country. Foreigners, if not excluded, were treated with suspicion, often watched by the police, and at times isolated from the people.

The political police first became prominent when the *Oprichnina* of Ivan the Terrible carried around a dog's head and broom as symbols of sniffing out treason and sweeping it away. It has never left the Russian scene, although it has gone slack from time to time. Such early tsars as Ivan the Terrible and Peter were ready to kill tens of thousands to eliminate those suspected of evil intentions and to cow the remainder, and Paul, at the end of the eighteenth century, struck down thousands. It was probably a sign of decreasing self-confidence that subsequent tsars shrank from mass slaughter even when threatened by real and violent revolutionary movements. Only in the aftermath of the near-overthrow of the government in 1905 were a few thousands executed.

Censorship was introduced into Russia along with printing and has always been in effect except briefly in the revolutionary breakdowns of 1905 and 1917. In the latter decades of tsardom, however, contacts with the West eroded it; and private ownership of a growing press enabled publishers and journalists to pit their wits freely against the censors. Authors could try to restate their message in a way which would slip by often unintelligent censors and so developed the technique of "Aesopian" expression. The tsarist state, not greatly concerned with public opinion and lacking a dynamic ideology, made little effort to give writers positive instructions.

The slogan was "Orthodoxy, Autocracy, Nationality," but the real ideology of the tsarist regime was orthodoxy. Rulers of premodern Western Europe tolerated an independent church not because they approved of it but because they were not in a position to subdue it, as Russian rulers were. The subjection of the Orthodox Church was completed by Peter, who placed the church under a synod of bishops named by himself. Subsequently, the church became practically a department of the state and shared its rot. Its chief function was to bless the social and political order, calling for obedience to the tsar and the payment of taxes. Religious instruction was mandatory in primary and secondary schools, and adherence to orthodoxy was a mark of belonging to the political community. Lacking stimulation for independent thought, the Orthodox Church became extremely conservative, dogmatic and formalist. The consequent weakness of religious faith in an atmosphere of intense religious emotion helped to nourish revolutionary utopianism.

Like the church, the Russian nobility was denied any autonomy faintly comparable to that of its counterparts in the West. Status depended theoretically not on birth but only on service to the state; anyone with proper qualifications should have been able to get onto the career ladder at the bottom and climb according to merit and ability to the highest grade of nobility. In fact, of course, the road to the top was short for those born to wealth and official connections and was nearly impossible for the vast majority of the population. But social mobility was higher than in many Western countries, and many a man rose from poverty to the highest standing. Nor was race a barrier; Turks or Tatars (if russified) had a fair chance.

Behind the notion of rank by service there was an ethos of the equality of all beneath the all-powerful tsar, who was in turn theoretically devoted to the welfare of his charges. It was considered excellent to be a servant, as all together were, of the master of the universe. Standing above classes, he was guardian of a kind of democracy, which in the tsarist as in the Soviet context meant social justice and equality. "We are all in state service," said Nicholas I, a martinet autocrat who boasted of the popular election of his dynasty. Autocracy was supposed to protect the humble and prevent the exploitation of man by man. Russians dreamed of a great collectivist state based on the loyal masses and the loving ruler.

In reality, the peasants, comprising the overwhelming mass of the population (nearly four-fifths as late as the revolution), were enserfed from the sixteenth century until the middle of the nineteenth, their condition worsening to virtual slavery at the same time that serfdom was coming to an end in Western Europe. The emancipation of 1861 failed to improve their lot greatly because of its onerous conditions.

Often driven to the edge of starvation by the tax-gatherer, they were vulnerable to extortion, subject to conscription which was not unlike a long penal servitude, usually regarded practically as cattle by haughty officials, and often flogged. Their rage and hostility, surging up in 1917, made the Bolshevik Revolution possible.

An equalitarian feature of the peasant commune, which many radicals admired and of which Karl Marx approved, was the periodic redivision of cropland. Cultivation was done by individual families, but within the commune ideas of individual property were weak. This was not, however, merely peasant mentality; property rights were generally less sacred in Russia than in the West. In line with the theory that all Russia was the estate of the ruler, private ownership was theoretically always conditional, although in practice reasonably secure. There was a feeling that powerful private interests were incompatible with the dignity of the state, and the idea of an aristocracy of wealth or a bourgeois political order was abhorrent. The tsarist empire, like other comparable empires, was anticapitalistic in spirit. Commerce was held in low esteem, and the merchant class was regarded for the most part as loathsome rascals. Foreign capital owned a large part of industry and mining, somewhat as in Latin America today. Xenophobia was added to hatred of the bourgeoisie to produce a climate conducive to Marxist radicalism.

The Russian middle and industrial classes were the weaker because much of the economy was government-owned or controlled. Much of the land belonged to the state or crown. The government built the railroads, largely managed foreign trade, and sponsored forced-draft industrialization primarily for military needs. At the end of the nineteenth century, nearly half of the large enterprises were state-owned, and most of the rest depended on state orders or official protection. Nationalization of industry by the Leninists represented no transcendent change.

The state-dominated economy was inefficient; Russia was much poorer than such lands as England, France, or Germany next door, despite abundant land and raw materials. This was not simply a matter of making up for the centuries of Mongol dominion. From the sixteenth century, the tsarist state fostered the importation of Western technology, at least so far as relevant to military needs. Peter the Great around the beginning of the eighteenth century made a herculean effort to industrialize and modernize in all ways, even requiring his subjects to shave and smoke. But his successors became rather complacent, and Russia tended to fall farther behind, especially when the industrial revolution accelerated in Europe in the nineteenth century. Only in the last decades of the tsarist state did Russia have another economic spurt.

The heart of the difficulty seems to have been that the Russian system was devised and directed primarily toward assuring political control, and economic considerations were sacrificed to political. For this reason and because officials' instincts for power and desires for gain were unchecked, Russian society was, from the point of view of economic development, overgoverned and overtaxed, controls and taxation lying most heavily on producers. Competition was seen as evil in principle. There were few incentives for improvement of production; political favor was the way to get ahead.

BREAKDOWN

Russia was able to use Western technology to subdue much of the East and thus to draw strength from empire to resist the West; but in so doing it encountered problems which in one form or another have plagued the Russian state and society to this day. Economic development was necessary for military strength, yet in the long run economic development was subversive to the authoritarian state, which was indispensable to hold the empire together. It was necessary to educate, but education raised up a class that demanded more freedom than the regime could countenance. It was necessary continually to borrow from the more inventive West, yet the state could never devise a perfect sieve to admit useful technical knowledge while excluding corrosive social and political ideas. It was impossible to take over much of Western civilization without being influenced by its political implications.

The clash of purposes and outlooks goes back to Ivan the Terrible, who imported Western technicians while crushing vestiges of independence among his servitors, some of whom longed for the freedom and constitutionalism of then-great Poland. It became far more acute as Peter westernized on a broad front. Thereafter, Russia was inseparable from Europe; and as it evolved from a simple society of rulers and serfs toward a complex pluralism with small middle and professional classes, a few writers and thinkers began nourishing libertarian ideas. After the exposure of large numbers of Russian soldiers to Western society in the Napoleonic wars, liberalism became something of an intellectual fad in the upper classes, and the tsar himself gave thought to a constitution. On the death of Alexander in December, 1825, a group of French-influenced officers attempted to impose a constitution by mutiny, an event later hallowed as the beginning of revolutionary actions in Russia. The abortive coup gave the tsarist government a fear of imported ideas, which the new tsar, Nicholas I, excluded so far as possible while keeping tight reins at home in rather Stalinist fashion. He thus kept Russia quiet for three decades at the cost of stagnation and decadence.

The response to defeat in the Crimean War was a series of liberalizing measures to patch up the old order, the most important of which was the freeing of the peasants in 1861 from semislavery. But no basic reform was possible, and discontents rose together with economic progress in the latter decades of the nineteenth century. The new factory workers, ex-peasants adrift in the cities, particularly felt the burdens of early industrialization and were correspondingly susceptible to radicalism. The peasants, called upon to finance industrialization by grain exports, as in later Soviet times, were frustrated in expectations of improvement. The nobility, the class upon which the regime saw itself resting, was becoming self-consciously useless and demoralized; many of its offspring became revolutionaries. At the same time, the more liberally-inclined classes were rising, not only the growing numbers of business managers, merchants, bankers, and the like, but nonbureaucratic professionals, lawyers, scientists, doctors, engineers, journalists, and teachers. Unlike bureaucrats, police, and soldiers, these people were not instruments of domination but were resistant to it.

The ideological foundations of the autocracy were also crumbling. The old messianism, with its universal vocation for Russia and the tsar, was becoming a bit absurd as Russia found itself playing the game of power politics on a level with other states and none too successfully. The ideas of autocracy, orthodoxy and nationality were equally eroded. Loyalty to a ruling house, particularly one which had produced no very inspiring personality since Alexander I, was no longer an adequate bond of empire. The doctrinally weak Orthodox Church was mystically backward and bureaucratically run, and shared the corruption of the government. The seminaries produced not only priests but many revolutionaries, such as Stalin.

The last element of the triad, nationality, was equally ineffectual. There could be no nationalism for the whole empire, which required a supranational or universalist basis. But nationalism, the basis of Western European states, could not be excluded. The Russians, who were less than half the population, began thinking of the empire less as a universal entity and more as a Russian possession. Beginning in the 1880's, russification, often harsh and crude, became official policy, especially against Poles, Ukrainians, and Jews. By the end of the empire, some of the minorities were dreaming of independence.

The increasingly, although somewhat superficially, westernized and educated sectors were almost unanimously desirous of great change, ashamed of the poverty of the peasants and the backwardness of the government. Suffering from inferiority to the West abroad and from their lack of status at home, many of them became passionately negative, rejecting the past and present of Russia even while moved by a great yearning for its renovation. The regime was consequently subjected in the latter part of the nineteenth century to a rising tide of criticism. The progress of journalism opened many more channels of expression and increased the problems of the censors. The expansion of higher education, required by the needs of bureaucracy and favored by the interests of the privileged classes, swelled the ranks of the unemployed or underemployed intellectuals. Many indulged in imbalanced and immature criticism and in daydreams of the perfect society. The main theme of the Slavophils, and subsequently of the Populists, was the traditional socialism of the peasant commune. Nihilism was for a time a fashion; in a semihysterical reaction against futility, eager youths talked about scrapping the old world without any clear idea of what they would put in its place. Often they were infatuated with science, seemingly the key to Western success. Yet in spirit they were the opposite of scientific. Their thought was as absolutist as their state, with no sense of qualified validity or of searching for truth by weighing conflicting evidence. They had no feeling for compromise or sense of the legitimacy of different political views, but thought in terms of black and white of a single vision of justice and order.

As the regime felt its moral foundations weakening, it sought to save itself by military victory, and so entered an unpopular war against Japan in 1904. Rapid and humiliating defeats brought popular protest, strikes, and demands for reform. After the massacre of about a thousand petitioners before the tsar's palace in January, 1905, discontent snowballed. Business leaders and professional men joined workers' demonstrations and strikes while peasants looted and burned. By October the country was paralyzed.

In the emergency, the tsar felt compelled to promise an elected legislative body and extensive civil rights, similar to those later enshrined in the Soviet constitution, freedom of speech and assembly, freedom from arbitrary arrest, and universal suffrage. This was a tactical success as it appeased the moderates, although the extremists sought to continue violent action. The armed forces remained generally loyal, and in 1906 the peasants were subdued, the strike movement was broken, and many leaders of discontent were driven abroad, exiled to Siberia, or executed.

The half-constitution was no success. The tsar and his entourage felt unable to permit any real restriction of the autocratic power, so they dissolved the first two Dumas, as the parliamentary body was called, when these tried to assert themselves. The manner of election was then changed to produce tame Dumas, which could neither control the ministry nor draw up legislation. Yet the Dumas served as a forum from which even radical parties like the Bolsheviks could present their views, and they encouraged the reformist and liberal currents in Russian society.

In general, the last peacetime years of the tsarist government saw increasing freedom, an increasing spirit of legality, a growing belief in individualism, a maturing, semifree critical press, and flourishing literature. With the rapid expansion of the liberal classes the old class structure was being left behind. There seemed to be some prospects that the Duma would gradually achieve more authority, just as Western European parliaments had in their historical evolution. There was a growing inclination to accept Russia's place as a member of the European state system instead of maker of universal order. The intellectuals were turning away from idealistic radicalism and apocalyptic visions to tackle practical problems or to seek the enjoyments of the day.

Modernization of the countryside was fostered by legislation in 1906 making it possible for peasants to demand separation of their holdings from the communal village and so to become independent farmers. Many of them hastened to do so, to the marked betterment of agriculture. A small-owner class was growing up as the world war began. Industrial development also resumed, with a larger role for private ownership. It is easily, although perhaps unfairly, calculated that if Russia could have kept up the growth rate of these years it would by now be at least as advanced as the Soviet Union after its series of five year plans.

But the political problem was not solved. The traditional autocracy was patently obsolete, and there was no apparent way it could be reformed or replaced. The growing business, professional, and working classes were certain to demand a place which tsarist prerogative could not allow. There was conflict of old and new values, a crudity of undigested change and uncertainty of direction akin to that seen in many less developed countries today. To educate was to raise a host of demands that traditional autocracy could not satisfy.

Yet the tsarist leadership was singularly unable to consider basic reforms. Change would have meant curtailment of their power; in the weakness of their position, they feared to make any concessions. There was never any theoretical retreat from the principle of absolutism. The government, whose only real supporters were the conservative bureaucrats who dominated it, was becoming more and more isolated. It was driven to such expedients as anti-Semitism and pogroms in order to enlist popular support, but these measures further alienated the intelligentsia and provided much Jewish leadership for the revolutionary movement.

Revolutionary change thus seems to have been unavoidable on the eve of the world war. For decades a Russian Revolution had been predicted on all sides, and the close call of 1905 seemed to confirm the expectations. Revolutions come not because people are poor and oppressed but because they begin to demand more, not from stagnation but from the breakdown of institutions and failure of adjustment. These were patent facts of 1913 Russia.

This does not mean bolshevism was in any sense inevitable. The very fact that radical revolution was widely foreseen made it less likely, and the 1905 semirevolution probably did not raise (as the Bolsheviks claimed) but lowered the readiness of the country for a violent attack on existing institutions. Then the army had saved the dynasty. In a future crisis, it might permit the Romanovs to be overthrown, but it would surely halt any revolutionary movement far short of the extremism of the Leninists. For these to come to power, it was indispensable that the regular military forces be effectively destroyed, which could occur only in an unsuccessful major war.

On the other hand, there is no basis for the assumption that, but for the world war and the opportunity it gave for an extremist movement like bolshevism to come to power, the Russian empire must have ripened into some sort of democratic state. The Russians were desirous of a constitution because it was a symbol of modernization and the autocracy was bankrupt, but they had little idea what representative government meant. It was not easy for them to learn, as the fissures in Russian society were too many and too grave. Not only was there an almost unbridgeable gap between westernized upper classes and the "dark people"; democracy must have meant fragmentation of authority and dissolution of the empire. Parliamentary government requires fairly high standards of civic morality, willingness to compromise, mutual respect for rights, toleration of differences, and agreement on fundamentals, all of which were strikingly absent.

A democratic empire, which the liberals proposed, is a contradiction in terms; and the least tractable of the problems a parliamentary Russia would face would be that of the differences of nationality, compounded by differences of religion. A Duma with dozens of parties representing dozens of nationalities, all desirous of more freedom, with a minority of Russians, could have produced only chaos. It was with reason that conservatives accused the liberals of proposing the dismemberment of the empire. The liberals had to base themselves on a false proposition, that Russia was basically like the West. If it were to follow the road to westernization to the end, it could only surrender the gains of centuries. But such a loss was and remains an unthinkable proposition to nearly all Russians.

The obvious alternative would have been a convulsion of disorders, some turnover of elites less cataclysmic than the Bolshevik Revolution, followed by a reassertion of strengthened authority. Any modernized Russian state would probably look in some ways like the Soviet Union of today. But it could hardly arrive at anything so strange to Russian tradition as Marxism-Leninism without the chain of events which led Lenin to the Kremlin.

FOOTNOTES

1.   There is a parallel to the Marxist eschatology whereby, after the fall of feudalism and capitalism, Moscow stands forth as the bearer of the new order of socialism.

CHAPTER 2

The Revolution

THE MOVEMENT

The radicals who became articulate after the middle of the nineteenth century looked to the West for ideas and theories, but their attitudes and ideals were Russian to the core, even if, like Herzen, Bakunin, or Lenin, they spent much of their lives abroad. Frustrated, unable to find a place in tsarist society, often with more education than could be gainfully employed, the revolutionaries of the 1870's or 1880's were typically dramatic and emotional, disposed to reject objectivity and balance. They sought an all-embracing truth, which was to dominate the whole world, a utopia somehow to be realized by violent exercise of the will. The core of their morality was the equalitarianism which the empire proclaimed but failed to bring about. Their creed was hatred for the bureaucracy and worship of the common people and their virtues as the salvation of Russia, if not of the universe. Somehow, the peasants should assert themselves, sweep away the evil old world, and make a new, perfect Russia.

The peasant commune as idealized by the Populists was a perfectly brotherly association, where all together enjoyed the fruits of their labors. This ideal, conceived primarily as an urge to moral-political rather than material well-being, was by no means strange to the tsarist

23

empire. This, in fact, was occasionally dubbed "communistic" by foreigners who were impressed by its emphasis on collectivity and equality, the fondness of Russians for the idea of socialism and their dislike of capitalism, the lack of sanctity of private property, the communalism of the peasant village, and the power of the tsar over persons and things. "The whole spirit of the old regime was collectivist in character."[1]

In the Russian popular culture there were recurrent tendencies to communism.[2] Land was commonly regarded as belonging properly to the tsar, so to God, or to the people in general. The sharing of property was a widespread ideal, at least of the discontented; it was sometimes broadened even to abolition of the family and communal child-rearing. Various sectarian groups, of whom the Dukhobors are best known, renounced ownership as evil and lived in more or less full communism. Russian emigrés abroad often formed little family-style communes. Lenin's party was less enthusiastic about this aspect of communism, as they focused attention on the prime questions of political power. But elemental popular drives for equal sharing, with bitter hatred of the privileged, provided emotional force behind the Bolshevik Revolution.

How society should be structured to assure brotherly equality was a question for which the revolutionaries had only the vaguest answers; when the old order was smashed, the new would be easy. Some looked to a strengthened autocracy as the instrument of their dreams. A good tsar should become a redeemer, instituting the utopian order of peace, justice, and equality among his children. Even when revolutionaries rejected the traditional rulership, their mentality was authoritarian. There was no place in their ideal state for individualism. All was to be for and by the great collective. The Populists saw constitutionalism as protector of wealth and privilege in the West. While promising ultimate freedom, they were quite willing, as Lenin later was, to contemplate a rather indefinite dictatorial power to perfect the new order.

The first idea of the revolutionaries was to raise up the people by propaganda. However, when the majority remained loyal to orthodoxy and the state, the movement became more elitist. As the majority did not support revolution, it should be made without them, if necessary against them; they would accept it afterwards. To make the new order, the elect had to be bound into a revolutionary organization. A pioneer in this direction and influential precursor of Lenin was Peter Tkachev, who stressed the need of a disciplined corps of intellectuals utterly devoted to the business of revolution to guide the masses. The revolutionaries turned to terrorism in the belief that picking off a few key oppressors would cause tsarist society to collapse. This campaign reached its climax in the assassination of tsar Alexander II in 1881. The result was the advent of a less enlightened tsar, who inaugurated severe repressions.

Thereafter, the revolutionary movement changed. The idea of raising the country by preaching seemed futile. Terror was no more successful, as the radical movement was broken up or pushed into obscurity by police action. The peasant commune itself was obviously decadent. A new intellectual influence from the West was also making itself felt in writings of a philosopher-economist not yet much celebrated in the West, Karl Marx, who argued that the essence of politics was class conflict and that the future belonged to the oppressed workers.[3]

From the uncertainty there emerged three main streams of radicalism. Some stayed faithful to the main directions of Populism although they retreated from its extremism. The peasants remained, after all, the large majority of the population and those whose wrongs most needed redressing. The neo-Populists in 1904 founded the Socialist-Revolutionary party, the main proposal of which was the "socialization" of the land, the fairly moderate proposal that those who actually worked the land should possess it. The party prospered, and in 1917 it had many more adherents than the Bolsheviks; but it lacked the unity and determination to contest Lenin's bid for power.

A more radical current was anarchism. In theory rejecting all government, anarchism was an emotional protest against the modernization which was beginning severely to erode traditional ways and values. The anarchists were too allergic to organization of any kind, even their own, ever to represent much of a positive political force. But, waving black flags and anathematizing the bourgeois, they were a great help to the Bolsheviks in tearing down the Provisional Government.

The Marxists represented a more moderate tendency. In the last decades of the tsarist government there was some recognition that change was likely to be slow. The intellectuals were losing faith in peculiar Russian virtues and wished to see Russia more a part of the modern world, sharing its values. In this situation, Marxism represented the most congenial train of Western thinking, and its influence rapidly spread.

The appeals of Marxism were multiple. It gave a reason to accept, as a progressive stage of history, the capitalistic industrial development which seemed inevitable; and it reconciled this acceptance with revolutionary spirit. It allowed radicals to look to the proletariat, when the peasantry failed, and gave a promise, based on elaborate theory, that the proletariat could not fail. Marx provided a coherent doctrine instead of the nebulous theories of his predecessors. He enjoyed the advantage of teaching "scientific socialism," supposedly based on the latest scientific learning of the West, at a time when science had boundless prestige. That Marxism was materialistic and antireligious delighted the almost unanimously antichurch Russian intelligentsia, and its comprehensiveness satisfied the yearning for a single answer to all questions. The Marxist could view himself as marching with the intellectual vanguard of humanity; and if Marxism was rejected by the West, the Russian who adopted it could feel himself the more progressive.

Marxism at the same time saved the long-suffering Russian self-respect. In its terms, backwardness was only a stage of economic development certain to be overcome. In the Marxist outlook, poverty was rather a virtue, as the Slavophils had told themselves, and wealth was the result of exploitation; if the West was rich, so much the worse for it. This is probably the chief reason that Marxism has found a large following among the educated and half-educated of countries irritated by contact with the technologically superior West down to the present time.

Marxism enjoyed another advantage in tsarist Russia in that the regime saw it as relatively harmless. It did not propose or authorize immediate revolution, for consistent Marxists warned that a premature attempt to bring socialism could only bring a new despotism. The rather dry theorizing of Marxism was not likely to stir the masses, and if the intellectuals entertained themselves with disputes about the stages of history, so much the better. The regime was pleased, also, that the main thrust of Marxism was not antitsarist but anticapitalistic and to a degree anti-Western. One cannot say that the government was mistaken, although it was eventually replaced by a Marxist party. The Bolsheviks had little to do with its demise, however successfully they stepped into the breach.

Many Marxists were as much concerned with bringing Russia up to Western levels as with leaping ahead into socialism. Others, following the revisionism which was current in Europe in view of the failure of Marxist prophecies, turned to economic issues and the struggle of the workers for improvement. In Russia as elsewhere, at the beginning of this century, Marxism was a decreasingly cogent creed of economic interpretation of history, subject to the erosion of a milieu in which capitalism was working fairly well and bringing material benefits to workers as well as owners. Among those who most bitterly fought against this tendency was the youngish Lenin, who polemicized at great length against all who would make Marxism less revolutionary.

LENINISM

Vladimir Ilyich Ulianov was born in Simbirsk, on the middle Volga, on April 22, 1870. His ancestry was mixed, Tatar and German with Russian. His background was nonproletarian; family affluence enabled him to spend his time ruminating on injustice and revolution. His father rose to district school inspector with a rank of hereditary nobility, equivalent to major general. Lenin once designated himself as "nobleman" on an official application. The traumatic event of his youth was the execution of his elder brother for participation in a plot to assassinate the tsar. He entered Kazan University to study law not long thereafter, but was soon involved in student disorders, arrested, and expelled. He obtained a law degree by private study but was barred from the normal ladder of official employment by his record. He began writing polemical pamphlets and took part in organizing Marxist circles among workers.

Ulianov was arrested in 1895 and sent, after fourteen months in jail, to exile in a Siberian village. There he acquired the pseudonym

"Lenin," taken apparently from the Lena river. Thanks to the books and papers he received, he spent his years of exile studying and writing. By the time of his return, in 1900, he seems to have come to the conviction that, just as the peasantry was no basis for a revolutionary movement, the proletariat left to itself tended to turn "petty bourgeois"; hence, socialism was to be brought by a revolutionary party.

From 1900 until 1905 and from 1907 until after the abdication of Nicholas II in 1917, Lenin remained abroad, writing and talking against the ameliorative approach toward which most intellectual leaders of Russian Marxism had drifted. Lenin recognized that it was necessary to adopt slogans popular with the workers, but he felt that any real effort to improve their living standards detracted from the basic political goal by reducing dissatisfactions. The workers, still loyal to the tsar, were more interested in rubles than revolution; to fill them with the proper class purpose, Lenin could look only to a firmly organized party, wholly dedicated to revolution. He directed himself to this theme in his seminal work, *What is to Be Done*, written in 1901-2, in which he characteristically elaborated not the beauties of socialism but the necessity of a cohesive party to guide the proletariat.

Lenin took the first steps toward building the kind of party he wanted when Russian Marxists gathered at Brussels (later transferring to London) in 1903 to organize the Russian Social Democratic Party. Lenin insisted that membership be limited to actual participants; his opponents were less exacting. The issue was outwardly small, but it was recognized as fundamental, dividing hard-liners and moderates. At one time, Lenin's faction became a majority and took the name of "Bolsheviks" (in Russian, "majorityites"), while their opponents were called "Mensheviks" ("minorityites"). This was a psychological advantage for the Leninists in succeeding years when they were more often than not actually in a minority.

However, Lenin, the determined architect of revolution, seems to have been confused and indecisive as the disorders of 1905 rose toward revolutionary violence. He returned to Russia only in November and did nothing of consequence, although for some weeks the tsarist government was practically paralyzed. When the government recovered powers, Lenin and other radical leaders ignominiously retreated abroad.

The following years were bleak. Throughout a long series of quarrels, Lenin was able to keep at his side only a minority of a minuscule party. He demanded above all firm unity, yet he could not keep his own faction united, and again and again he cast out dissidents rather than admit differences. Lenin remained, however, at the center of one wing of Russian Social Democracy, which became a separate party when he summoned a rump congress in 1912. The other intellectual leaders of Russian Marxism shunned it; their places were taken by faithful Leninists famous in later years, such as Kamenev, Zinoviev, and Stalin.

Bolsheviks and Mensheviks diverged on many issues. While the former wanted a narrow, conspiratorial party, the latter wanted to draw in more members of different shades of opinion and to work more openly. The former were willing to use funds acquired by banditry ("expropriations," some planned by Stalin); the latter were scandalized. The Bolsheviks damned the liberal bourgeoisie; the Mensheviks would work with liberals against the autocracy. Lenin's faction hoped for an early revolution; the Mensheviks thought that socialism could come only when Russia was ripe for it. The essence of the difference, in terms popular at the time, was "consciousness" versus "spontaneity." In other words, the Leninists wished to use Marxism for the making of revolution in Russia; their opponents wished to apply Marxism to the development of socialism in Russia.

MARXISM REVISED

Lenin had to modify the theories of the master to inspire revolutionary action in Russia, a country for which they were not intended and whose conditions were quite different from those which Marx analyzed. He rationalized that employment of any kind of violent opposition to the tsarist government was necessary for revolutionary purposes. The means of this violent opposition was, in the first instance, the peasantry. Marx had paid little attention to the peasants, who did not fit his general scheme; but Lenin saw their revolutionary potential as indispensable for the overthrow of the social order in an agrarian country. To square this with Marxist theory, Lenin looked to the developing differentiation of the villages and found landless agricultural laborers and the poorest peasants to be a kind of growing proletariat, giving Russia a proletarian majority. Those who hired a few hands and owned several horses were called "capitalists."

Lenin also wished to make use of nationality discontent, but without conceding the substance of national independence. For Marxists generally, nationalism was a negative force, a nuisance and hindrance to desirable economic and political integration. Lenin thoroughly shared this view, but saw the immense desirability of enlisting the minorities of the Russian empire in his struggle. For this purpose he promised them, to the chagrin of many Social Democrats, complete independence. He insisted, however, that the party must be entirely centralized. The party, then, remained free to oppose the exercise of the theoretical right of secession if a nationality should be so misled as to ask for it. This ability to grant the form while denying the substance of independence helped the Bolsheviks to win the civil war. It later became the keystone of the nationality policy of the Soviet Union.

Lenin also devised a passably Marxist rationalization for the making of revolution in Russia. This country, although not comparable in underdevelopment to most of Asia and Africa, was generations away from the overripe capitalism the breakdown of which should usher in the age of socialism. It was central to the Marxian understanding of history that a new form of society should be based on new means of production, not political action. But Lenin propounded that the proletariat, aided by the peasantry, should help to make the bourgeois revolution and then make its own proletarian revolution, practically skipping over the stage of capitalism.

Lenin also justified revolution in Russia by a more basic revision of Marxism, one which greatly added to its appeal not only for Russia but for all less developed lands. According to his theory of imperialism, latter-day capitalism saves itself from overproduction, crises, and class warfare by exporting surplus capital, exploiting colonial territories, and using part of the booty to bribe the native working class. This explained why the socialist revolution had failed to arrive in Europe as expected by Marx. More important, it put exploited countries almost in the place of an exploited proletariat. Although imperial Russia, an underdeveloped importer of capital, was a living refutation of his own approach, Lenin saw his country as exploited victim of the foreign capital which figured so largely in its economy. Russia, then, should be a good country in which to begin the world socialist revolution. Lenin, like Marx, believed that the revolution would have to be international; but Russia, as he put it, was the weakest link of world capitalism.

This meant that, in a reversal of Marxism, the correct degree of backwardness was an advantage for the building of something to be called socialism. But this required that the revolution be made not by an economic class but by a political organization. However much he stressed the "dictatorship of the proletariat," Lenin had no faith in the proletariat's knowing its own will. For Marx, the workers should develop class consciousness from their struggle and conditions; Lenin insisted they must be taught it by bourgeois intellectuals, since, "The history of all countries shows that the working class, exclusively by its own effort, is able to develop only trade-union consciousness . . ."[4] The proletariat must be led by a disciplined, secret, semimilitary organization of dedicated revolutionaries.

This role of the party meant that workers were to be led not by men from their own ranks but by a self-appointed group of non-working-class origins. It was difficult for a genuine proletarian to find time to become a professional revolutionary, as a Bolshevik should be. The party leadership of the Bolsheviks (and other radical groups) was of the middle or upper class background which made possible leisure and education. Few indeed were the outstanding Bolsheviks of humble birth; and these, like Stalin, took little part in party councils in exile. Although exalting the proletariat, Leninism in reality gave a mission to the discontented bourgeois intelligentsia.

As the party became something of a religious entity, deriving its authority not from consent but from its possession of truth, democracy was excluded. The Bolsheviks had to stand for minority rule in a land whose industrial proletariat was no more numerous than the nobility, and the enormity of the task of bringing a socialist revolution to a relatively backward peasant country justified overriding majority will.

Hence Lenin made much of the idea of dictatorship of the proletariat, a concept which Marx had used but had not elaborated. It was the duty of the party, representing the proletariat, to grasp power as best it could and retain it by the means necessary.

THE LENINIST STYLE

Lenin's political ideas were part of his forceful personality. Intolerant of differences of opinion, he rushed to attack anything that smelled to him like doctrinal deviation. From the first, most of his writings were directed not at the old regime but against those who shared his professed goals but favored different approaches. He vacillated a good deal in his theoretical formulations according to political needs, but the unifying core of his thought was the necessity of revolution. The truth of Marxism, as Lenin saw it, was whatever advanced his cause. Thus in 1906 as in 1917 he approved of the workers' councils ("soviets") when they seemed to be useful to the Bolsheviks and turned his back on them when they seemed less propitious. He instructed the Bolsheviks to denounce the liberals yet to take advantage of cooperation with them. He was rather candid in demanding agitation for benefits for workers and peasants only to cultivate revolutionary sentiments, as in clamoring for universal suffrage while despising parliaments. Lenin held force to be an acceptable means to the supreme end, if not actually preferable for its decisiveness; he had no patience for any argument that socialism might be brought about by gradual or peaceful action. His supreme strategy was the party organization.

Lenin's political ideas were in the traditional Russian mold. During his long stay abroad, he lived spiritually in Russia and formed few associations and no friendships with Westerners. A great internationalist in theory, he was wholly preoccupied with the destiny of Russia. For him, as for Dostoievsky, Europe was decadent; Russia was to save it.

Lenin's political organization was also in the Russian mode. There was some European precedent for an elite party, like the Jacobins of French revolutionary times, but the ordinary political party in Western practice was a very loose and open affair, and it was taken for granted that Marxist Social-Democratic parties should be mass-based. Lenin went back to the conspiratorial style of the Populist revolutionary-terrorists. His excuse for secrecy and narrowness was the difficulty of operation under police repression, but the police had no difficulty in penetrating the Bolsheviks, or any other antiregime organizations. In 1917 and after, the ruling party retained its elitist conspiratorial style. The idea that a few should act on behalf of the passive masses was inherent in Lenin's mentality, as it was in that of the bureaucratic empire.

Leninism shared with the Populists a desire for secrecy, a willingness to use violence (on a "class," instead of individual basis), and a dislike for the middle classes which capitalism was raising up. Lenin was also at one with the Populists in seeking an early socialist revolution. They wished to skip the capitalist stage by reverting to the peasant commune. Lenin wanted to abbreviate Russian capitalism by revolutionizing the proletariat in alliance with the peasantry.

The tsarist state created favorable conditions for Bolshevism. Its repressiveness justified extremism on the part of its opponents and gave respectability to their violence of language and program. The repression of trade-unions and strikes prevented the growth of organizations dedicated to material betterment and was the best evidence for the Leninists' argument that the workers should look to political, not economic, goals. Trends in the decade before World War I were, however, unfavorable to the Leninist approach. Prosperity was eroding the morale of revolutionary parties. If socialist ideas were percolating in the growing working class, the intellectuals were turning away. Increased freedom of discussion within Russia further discouraged extremism. Bolshevism seemed to pertain more to the past than to the future of Russia; in 1914 the party was practically a shambles.

Because of its narrowness, Lenin's party could not achieve much in normal conditions. But in a fluid and uncertain situation calling for leadership to impose order and direction, none was as well prepared to grasp the helm as Lenin and his followers.

1917

Plagued by unrest, the Russian government was not displeased to go to war in 1914. In the ensuing patriotic enthusiasm, strikes and clashes with police ceased immediately, and revolutionary parties were reduced to insignificance. But the Russian army was severely battered by the Germans from the beginning of the war. Defeats discredited the autocracy, a *raison d'etre* of which was military strength. The reliable and well trained officers and troops were replaced by increasingly unreliable recruits. Munitions ran short. A growing stream of deserters and draft dodgers filled the cities with outlaws who had the strongest interest in the downfall of the regime. Production and earnings slumped, while prices skyrocketed, and a few grew rich while many hungered. Strikes multiplied. By the beginning of 1917 the police were increasingly unable to check violence.

Thus put on trial, the regime demonstrated astonishing incapacity. The shallow Nicholas lost touch with everyone outside his family. In September, 1915, he dutifully went off to the front to assume responsibility; the empress and the sinister monk, Rasputin, took charge in the capital. Everything was done to alienate the moderates; the government showed itself more concerned with its monopoly of authority than with winning the war. Rumor had it that the court was pro-German and the conviction grew that it was an obstacle to victory. Controls began breaking down. In March, 1917, riots in the capital grew beyond the capacity of the police and troops were called upon to suppress them. But the soldiers turned on their officers instead. The generals then decided that Nicholas must go, and he quietly bowed out.

With the age-old autocracy gone, there was a veritable intoxication of liberty undampened by appreciation of the enormous difficulties of building the new and juster state which everyone awaited. The new Russia would find new strength for the war, as all joined in defense of liberty. All parties came together in rare harmony. Even the Bolsheviks, much weaker than Mensheviks and Socialist-Revolutionaries, lent half-hearted support to the new Provisional Government and its policy of carrying on the war.

But the self-designated Provisional Government was never effective. The autocrat was the only national symbol and center of power; upon his removal, the situation was basically anarchic. A group of Duma leaders came together to form a sort of cabinet to keep order and carry on the business of the nation pending the election of a constituent assembly. But theirs was an unsubstantial government which could operate only with the acquiescence of the Petrograd (St. Petersburg having been Slavicized in the war) Soviet. In a replay of 1905, this body sprang into existence with alacrity when the old authority vanished. At the instance of some leftists and labor officials, Petrograd workers elected some 500 delegates, who were joined by about 2,000 delegates of the local garrison. The fact that it was in reality mostly representative of the army gave the Petrograd Soviet (and others like it arose rapidly all over Russia) special strength. The Soviet immediately took over some functions of government, such as food distribution and the establishment of a militia; and its decrees were more persuasive for workers and soldiers than those of the recognized government.

Despite this, the Socialist-Revolutionaries and Mensheviks who dominated the Soviet did not believe the day of socialism had dawned and refused to try to take control. Only the "bourgeoisie," they felt, could rule; but they set themselves the task of checking the Provisional Government, severely reducing its ability to act. Thus for several months there were two rather contrary political powers in the land, the one unprepared and the other unable to grapple with the pressing issues of the war, land reform, economic ruin, and the institution of a constitutional regime.

Into this fluid situation Lenin dropped as a catalyst of change. He had spent the war in Switzerland, with little knowledge of what was going on at home and without much hopes of action. Shortly before the tsar's abdication he told a Swiss audience, "We of the older generation may not live to see the decisive battles of the coming revolution."[5] He could not return immediately after the tsar's abdication because the Allied Powers were reluctant to facilitate the travel of an antiwar agitator; at length, arrangements were made for him, with a number of other socialists, to traverse Germany.

Arriving in Petrograd on April 16, Lenin was greeted as a fellow-socialist by the president of the Soviet, who expressed the hope that he would join in the defense of newly-free Russia. Lenin instead turned to his own followers with a call for revolutionary action, and a few days later he promulgated his intransigently radical "April Theses": all power to be exercised by the Soviets; police, army, and bureaucracy to be abolished; a national bank under the Soviets to control the economy; confiscation of private landholdings; etc.

Lenin's propositions rapidly came to seem less wild as Russia drifted into chaos. Workers and peasants began claiming the benefits they had expected from the revolution, workers striking or seizing plants as peasants were taking private land. Production continued to fall and inflation accelerated. Friction increased between the Soviet and the Provisional Government, which was unwilling to subordinate itself to a body representing only workers, soldiers, and leftist political leaders. The Provisional Government could not bring itself to fill rapidly its legitimating function, the calling of an assembly to write a constitution. In July it tried to revive the spirits of the army and the nation by launching a grand offensive, but it reaped a disastrous defeat.

Meanwhile, Lenin's party grew amazingly. At the time of the tsar's overthrow, it was one of the smaller parties, with about 20,000 members; but by June, the Bolsheviks had a majority in the workers' section of the Soviet. Street demonstrations were taking a strongly Bolshevik coloring. Early in July, there were confused anarchist and pro-Bolshevik riots in Petrograd. The government was able to restore order, and in so doing it blamed the Bolsheviks for insurrection. Evidence was produced to show that Lenin was in the hire of the Germans, the party was partially suppressed, a number of leaders were arrested, and Lenin went into hiding in nearby Finland. However, the party was set back little; growth of Bolshevik membership and organizations continued to be rapid. The defeated army practically fell apart, the economy kept sliding downward in disorganization, and there was less to eat in freedom than there had been under the tsar. The reaction of conservatives to deepening crisis was to look to military dictatorship. At the beginning of September the front commander, Gen. Kornilov, was encouraged to move on the capital, displace the regime, and hang the radicals. Kerensky, head of the Provisional Government, alarmed, called upon all socialists, including the Bolsheviks, to join in repulsing the attempted coup. Bolshevik leaders were released, and arms were given to their Red Guards who had been drilling in the factories. Kornilov's soldiers refused to fight for him, and Kerensky was temporarily saved, but he could no longer control the mounting Bolshevik strength in the capital.

A few days after the Kornilov affair, the Petrograd and other major soviets, with their fluid membership, went over to the Bolsheviks. Lenin, fretting underground, began calling insistently on his party to seize power. The more cautious men of the Central Committee in Petrograd held back in fear that an attempted coup without broader support of the country could only lead to civil war if not reactionary military dictatorship. But under Lenin's bombardment of demands for early action, the committee agreed, in the middle of October, to authorize preparations for an uprising. Two of Lenin's longtime cohorts, Kamenev and Zinoviev, dissented so strongly that they attacked the decision in a non-Bolshevik paper, a sin to be held against them long afterward.

The chief means of the Leninists to power was their influence with the soldiers, who, if disinclined to fight for Bolshevism, were even less disposed to defend the Provisional Government. The Bolsheviks dominated the military committees which were set up at the time of the Kornilov episode and which they refused to disband afterwards. The Red Guards, undisciplined and poorly armed but increasingly numerous, drilled and talked of fighting capitalists. And sailors of the Baltic fleet were the most reliable Bolshevik force of all.

In October, rumors were flying that the government was preparing to abandon Petrograd or that the garrison of the capital would be sent to the front. In this atmosphere, the Bolshevik-dominated Petrograd Military Revolutionary Committee, headed by Trotsky, asserted authority over the garrison of the city; and the soldiers acknowledged that authority on November 3-4. The insurrection was practically complete thereby. On November 6, the government, belatedly striking back, tried to close Bolshevik newspapers, summon more reliable troops, and arrest Bolshevik leaders; but its orders had little effect. The Bolshevik leadership proceeded to carry out plans for occupation of strategic points and the seat of government, the tsars' old winter palace. There was little resistance or bloodshed; no one but a few cadets and a women's battallion was prepared to risk death for the Provisional Government.

The Bolsheviks probably did not have to make the insurrection in order to gain power. The Second Congress of Soviets was to meet on November 7. In it the Bolsheviks could count on a majority; and Lenin could then have acted in the name of the Soviets with much less risk and less divisively. But Lenin preferred a violent and dramatic overthrow, as called for by the ideology of class warfare and revolution. Since then, the Soviet Union has enormously glorified the events of these days, and the picture of armed workers storming the fortresses of capitalism has become part of the mythology of Leninism. Lenin also wanted the new era of history to be inaugurated not by the soviets but by his party. It was a party action, and although the party made a gesture of presenting power to the Congress of Soviets on the night of November 7, 1917, it has retained power firmly in its own hands ever since.

WHY LENIN WON

Before November 7, few contemplated that the Bolsheviks could take power, much less hold it. But in retrospect it is not difficult to understand the advent of Leninism. In critical and difficult times, extremists come to the fore; and Russia in 1917 was in deepest confusion. Lenin's party was strong in its power orientation, dedication to its cause, and corresponding ruthlessness. The Bolsheviks throve in a disorganized society needing integrating leadership.

Having stressed organization for years in exile, Lenin had the nucleus of a formidable political machine, while rival groups were more like debating societies. It meant much more to be a Bolshevik than to belong to a looser, less deeply committed Menshevik, Socialist-Revolutionary or other group. In September and October, when adherents of other parties tended to fall away in indifference and confusion, the

Bolsheviks held together. Bolshevik strength also derived from semimilitary discipline and structure. No other party had its own militia in 1917, and the Leninists proved skilled in working with and organizing military forces.

Thanks to the organizational coherence of his party and its dedication to an overriding goal, Lenin could be pragmatic and opportunistic without dividing and alienating his followers. He took over the slogans of land for the peasants and freedom for the minorities with little regard to what had seemed the imperatives of Marxism. He was also quick to perceive the utility of the soviets as a means through which Bolsheviks might first challenge the Provisional Government and then legitimize their own rule.

The removal of tsarist authoritarianism left a political vacuum waiting to be filled by a new authority, and only Lenin seemed determined to rule. The monarchists and conservatives were discredited and demoralized after the fall of the tsar. The liberals, Constitutional Democrats, and others were too divided, insufficiently demagogic, and too scrupulous to bid strongly for power. Russia was hardly riper for a democratic than for a socialist state. The people had no understanding of or feeling for parliamentary government, and their initial enthusiasm quickly faded as life grew worse instead of better in the new freedom. The middle classes and independent forces of society, the foundations of constitutional government, were impotent. The Provisional Government was a self-chosen body which pretended to rule while sailors and sundry extremists and rowdies marauded—a government unable to grapple with the big issues, to convoke a Constituent Assembly, even to act firmly in its own defense. Non-Bolshevik socialists were inhibited from assuming power because they felt, with reason, that the time was not ripe for a socialist state. The Socialist-Revolutionaries lacked a clear program, coherent organization, and a firm social base in the cities. The anarchists were anarchic. The Mensheviks held to the doctrinaire position they had long argued, that it was their duty only to check the "bourgeois" government, not to try to cheat history by replacing it.

The Bolsheviks profited also from their label of socialists. Socialism was supposedly the opposite of tsardom. A socialist autocracy was hard to conceive, as none had been known to exist, although Lenin had given warning enough of the "dictatorship of the proletariat." Marxists, Mensheviks, and others saw reason to fear only class enemies or reactionaries. Most people were confident that the Bolsheviks were too impractical to form a government in any case. Not even Lenin could have been aware of the potentialities of one-party government.

From a Marxist point of view, Bolshevik rule was ridiculous. The propertied classes, peasant-capitalists, landlords, merchants, managers, etc., were some 16% of the population, industrial workers only 2.5%. But Lenin's program coincided with broad Russian aspirations, emotions coming to the surface in a time of crisis. One of these was the urge of the peasants for land. They had repeatedly shown a disposition to rampage when controls were removed, and the socialization of landholding was a general demand although the holdings of the gentry had shrunk to less than a quarter as much as peasant holdings by 1914. Peasants turned factory workers or soldiers carried with them their urge for social justice and communalism and wanted "socialism," by which they understood equality, dignity for the poor, expropriation of the wealthy, and anticommercialism. All leftist parties favored some kind of workers' control or socialization of industry. However, only Lenin's followers felt free to encourage the workers to assert themselves without concern for the effects on production, just as they were uninhibited in calling on the peasants to seize land.

The Bolshevik appeal to collectivism and distrust for property was mingled with and overshadowed by the appeal to end a futile war which was presented as slaughter in the interests of landowners and capitalists or Western capitalist-imperialists. The effort to continue fighting (upon which the Western allies were adamant) was fatal for the Kerensky government. Lenin's peace propaganda helped destroy the main force which might still have kept the Bolsheviks from power; they were lifted to the top by hordes of soldiers and ex-soldiers anxious not to be sent to the front.

Rejection of "bourgeois" values and antiwar agitation merged into antiwesternism and Russian messianism garbed in Marxism. In disorder and defeat, Lenin proclaimed a Russian world mission of overthrowing the old order and leading mankind into the new era of freedom, justice and socialism in the name of the oppressed and suffering peoples. Russia, beaten in the war, undertook the glorious task of ending all wars; bent in exhaustion, she should become teacher and savior of all. This comforting messianism was coupled with a utopianism as attractive as it was visionary. The new era of universal peace and justice should mean, in the Bolshevik message, the end of the hated institution of the state itself, eventually (in common belief, very soon) the end of money, and the inauguration of brotherly community of goods. The Leninists offered not a change of government but a dream, or many dreams: land for peasants, workers' control of industry, freedom for minorities, rule of the underprivileged, and above all peace. Their advent to power ushered in the contrary: long years of conflict and hardships beyond any Russia had suffered for centuries. But they gave it an effective government.

FOOTNOTES

1. Bernard Pares, *My Russian Memoirs* (J. Cape, London, 1931), p. 52.

2. Russia was not exceptional in this regard; authoritarian empires have frequently generated demands for the sharing of material goods. Their people feel cheated of promised equality and justice and see wealth as the product of corruption and rapacity of officials. Rights of private ownership are somewhat indistinct, while everything ultimately belongs to the godlike ruler, by implication to the whole body of the people. With little idea of individualistic democracy or constitutional restrictions of power, reformers conceive not a free society in the Western sense but an ordered and integrated society of equalitarian justice, equal duties, and equal access to the goods of earth. They would not destroy the autocratic system but perfect it. As Herzen remarked a century ago, "Communism is Russian autocracy turned upside down."

3. For a discussion of Marxism see pp. 85-88.

4. Lenin, "What is to be Done," Samuel Hendel, ed., *The Soviet Crucible* (D. Van Nostrand Co., Inc., Princeton, N.J., 1959), p. 131.

CHAPTER 3

Lenin's State

TOWARD POLITICAL MONOPOLY

Lenin announced to the assembled toilers of the Congress of Soviets, "We will now proceed to build the socialist order." No one then could say what the socialist order would look like nor how long would be required to complete the revolution. It was only after more than two decades that the Soviet state settled into the form given it by Stalin.

Those decades were eventful and complicated, but one theme dominates the political development of the whole period: the elimination of competition and dissent. When Lenin took hold of the reins in 1917, there were many freely operating political parties, and hardly anyone thought in terms of single party government, much less one party's monopoly of political action. There was a free press and no political police. Local soviets did as they pleased. In 1917, even Lenin's party was accustomed to debate and differences of opinion; it would have seemed absurd to speculate that one day comrades might be punished for slightly dissident views.

By the time Stalin had consolidated his power with the great purges of 1936-38, not only was the press reduced to an echo of official policy; art and literature were brought to servility. Industry and agriculture had been put under the most highly centralized control ever known. A breath of opposition to the will of the leader, sometimes even of luke-warmness, was an invitation to forced labor or death at the hands of a political police which had grown to be one of the major powers in the state.

The first step of this transformation was Lenin's decision to have the party carry out the overthrow of Kerensky without waiting for the Congress of Soviets to sanction it. The next came in the putting-together of a government. It was widely assumed that there should be a coalition of socialist parties; Mensheviks and Socialist-Revolutionaries warned that an attempt by the Bolsheviks to set up a one-party government could only lead to civil war. Many or most Bolsheviks agreed; only Lenin and a few next to him seem to have thought in terms of unshared Bolshevik power. The force of opinion compelled Lenin to enter nego-tiations with the other socialist parties, but he had his way, and an all-Bolshevik Council of Commissars was set up—the word "commissar" being a tribute to the propensity of Russian revolutionaries to think of theirs as a sequel to the French Revolution. The government was somewhat broadened in a few days, however, by the inclusion of Left Socialist-Revolutionaries, a leftist offshoot of the old peasant party. They were useful because they had a strong basis in the countryside, but there was never a question of real sharing of power, and the coali-tion broke up after a few months. It was also made clear that power was not to go to the Soviets, however useful the slogan. The first de-crees were passed practically without debate or opposition, and the congress was sent home.

Setting up an administration was harder. The new commissars were experienced agitators with few notions of administration. Most gov-ernment officials went on strike. But they gradually resumed work, for lack of choice; life under bolshevism was not so bad as feared, as Lenin was quite willing to use them. In late November, elections to the Con-stituent Assembly were permitted (against Lenin's will) to go forward as planned. The Bolsheviks were unable to do much toward influencing the results, at least in the countryside where the mass of peasants were indifferent to Marxism; and they won only a quarter of the votes. When the assembly long and loudly demanded by all revolutionary parties met in January, the Bolsheviks simply dissolved it. Three days later a new Congress of Soviets met and declared itself a permanent government. Lenin contended that the workers (and by extension their Bolshevik vanguard) were under no obligation to bow to a peasant majority in view of the class backwardness of the latter. Most remarkable, however, was the general indifference to something which had seemed so vital a few months earlier.

One of Lenin's first acts in power was to curb the press, closing nonsocialist papers and subsequently non-Bolshevik socialist ones. This reversal of a long-held socialist position was shocking to some of the more idealistic Bolsheviks and contributed to the crisis of the first days of the new government. From the beginning, the Leninists also began dissolving, disrupting, or taking control of uncooperative organizations, including numerous trade-unions friendly to the Mensheviks. They did this by persuasion, by mobilizing minorities or forming rump or competing organizations, or by coercion. Opposition was treated practically from the outset as sabotage and class betrayal.

In December a secret police was formed, the Special Commission ("Cheka," from its Russian initials), to take over the functions of the tsarist Okhrana. Within a few weeks it was arresting Menshevik and Socialist-Revolutionary leaders, as well as executing "counterrevolutionaries."

The Bolsheviks began rapidly also to reshape institutions, making the revolution more and more difficult to reverse. One of the first (and most popular) moves was ending private property in land, in a sense returning to the old Muscovite system whereby all land was property of the ruler. To feed the cities without giving the peasants much in return, the forcible requisition of grain was begun, and a state monopoly of grain was instituted. Foreign trade was put under a state monopoly. Banks were nationalized, a vital step not only in view of Lenin's estimate of the importance of finance capital but also a practical measure to deprive oppositionists of funds. Workers' control of factories was decreed, but this at first meant little more than a sanctioning of previous practice. Formal nationalization of most plants was decreed in June, 1918, and the government gradually took over administration.

There was a cascade of social-political changes. The Orthodox Church was separated from the state and then deprived of the right to hold property and to conduct religious education. The old legal system was for a time practically cast aside. Marriage and family laws were loosened, although Lenin, a man of rather bourgeois manners, had no liking for proposals that the family be dissolved and children raised in common.

Although the revolution had spread over the country with remarkable ease—Moscow exceptionally saw about a week's fighting—the authority of the central government was at first tenuous. Local soviets thought the new freedom meant managing their own affairs, and in the general confusion the authorities in Petrograd could not do much to check them. The state itself should cease soon to exist, many thought, or be swallowed up in a world socialist community. Or else Soviet power was sure to be overthrown. No Marxist could imagine the socialist revolution enduring in Russia alone; Lenin is said to have leaped with joy when he noticed that his government had outlasted the seventy-one days of the Paris Commune.

The Bolsheviks turned seriously to the building of a new state only in March, 1918, when by accepting the Peace of Brest-Litovsk they in effect admitted that world revolution might be delayed. German peace terms, severing the (non-Russian) Baltic area and the Ukraine, seemed unbearably severe; and a majority of Bolsheviks, not to speak of all other parties, were passionately opposed to acceptance. The Brest-Litovsk decision was the last issue really subject to debate in the party. Until the latter 1920's party men could speak out in party congresses, but never again was the outcome in doubt. The debate over ratification in the Congress of Soviets was similarly the last real debate in the theoretically sovereign body.

At this time, Lenin took two other notable steps. The seat of government was moved from Petrograd to Moscow and its ancient Kremlin, as Petrograd was dangerously exposed to the German advance. The motive was strategic, but it seemed to symbolize a reversal of the Western orientation of Russia ever since Peter had acquired his window on the Baltic. Lenin also changed the name of the party from "Social Democratic" to "Communist," to differentiate his party from the allegedly revisionist Marxist parties of Western Europe, "social patriots," as he termed them.

In July the Bolsheviks' onetime allies, the Left S.R.'s, rose in protest against the peace with Germany. When they were quickly crushed, the Bolshevik party monopoly was made absolute. Menshevik and Socialist-Revolutionaries had already been expelled from the soviets as anti-Soviet. The anarchists were broken, too, as they had become a nuisance. Some non-Bolshevik groups were allowed to function in the civil war as long as they cooperated, but after July, 1918, political competition was outlawed. In August, Lenin was wounded by a would-be assassin, and the Cheka was loosed for the indiscriminate Red Terror against "class enemies."

CIVIL WAR

The insurrection of the Left S.R.'s marked the beginning of a new period of conflict and turmoil lasting for some three years. The struggle was confused, complicated by interventionist efforts of Russia's former allies, an army of Czech ex-prisoners, and the aspirations of many minorities for independence from both Communist and anti-Communist Russians. At times as many as twenty independent political authorities claimed the government of all or part of the former empire.

The Whites, who included monarchists, democrats, and anti-Bolshevik socialists, had the advantages of foreign support and the inheritance of military skills of the old army. Those of the Reds included antiforeignism—the ineffective Western intervention was presented as the real enemy—and the semimilitary discipline of the party. The ranks of the party swelled as it called upon Russian patriotism, and they served as reliable shock troops to rush in wherever need was most dire. Lenin and Trotsky overcame the lack of Bolshevik officers and built up a fairly effective new Red Army by hiring or drafting tsarist officers, with Bolshevik commissars placed next to them to guard against disloyalty.

The anti-Bolshevik conservatives, moderates, and socialists were often not on speaking terms; and as the generals took charge in the warfare, liberals and democrats dropped out. Many saw little reason for choosing between left and right, as the two sides were about equally violent, terroristic, and dictatorial. The Leninists were held together by purpose and ideology. The Bolsheviks promised a socialist paradise, while their opponents held out hopes of little more than a return to the past. The anti-Communists had very little to put in place of the Bolshevik answers to the grave questions of the hour, such as the organization of the economy and land tenure; peasants feared their victory would mean return of the landlords. The issue of the minorities of the Russian empire most handicapped the White leaders. As Russian nationalists, they felt bound to uphold "Russia one and indivisible." But this was anathema to minority peoples; and the Whites were operating from peripheral, or mostly minority areas of the empire. Lenin dealt very neatly with the nationality problem. Immediately after the revolution he proclaimed the equal freedom of all peoples of the empire, including freedom of secession. At first he assumed that the peoples given freedom would no longer feel oppressed and so would not want to secede. When this was belied by a rush to independence of a dozen areas, the Bolsheviks insisted that all areas should have Soviet-style governments dominated by their party, that the only liberation they needed was from capitalists, bureaucrats and landlords. Russia, on the other hand, gained greatly in self-esteem by changing from master-nation of an empire into leader of the grand movement of supposedly free peoples, a higher unity in a glorious destiny. The fact that the Bolsheviks held the capital at all times, while they pointed to Allied assistance to anti-Bolshevik movements, White or nationalistic, in outlying regions, made their cause more convincing. Tsarist officers could accept the Bolsheviks as the party capable of restoring the Russian empire; and many fought voluntarily for their cause, even against other tsarist officers in White forces. When Soviet Russia in 1920 fought newly independent Poland, tsarist officers joined with nationalistic enthusiasm. They were doubtless right; only a very strong creed such as bolshevism could have held together the old conglomerate of peoples. The Leninists, from the standpoint of Russian greatness, deserved to win.

THE LENINIST SYNTHESIS

The Communist party came out of the ordeal hardened and strengthened, proud of having defeated alone the forces (as it claimed) of world capitalism. It had become a more militant and semimilitary body, accustomed to sole command and vindicated in its authority. But the country was in a shambles. The civil war plus the revolution and World War I were calamity enough; to these were added an administrative effort to implement total economic controls for which the regime was unprepared and the loss of most of the former educated classes through war, emigration, terrorism, and hardship. Agricultural production was down to half and industrial production to a fifth of prewar levels. Transportation was at a standstill. The hungry cities had lost half their population, wages were down to about a third. The peasantry was in revolt against the grain requisitions, now that there was no longer fear of the landowners' reclaiming their properties; and in March, 1921, the Kronstadt sailors, successors of those who had once been the Bolsheviks' best supporters, rose in revolt. Controls had so broken down that almost half the cities' food supply went through the black market.

Lenin's answer, in the spring of 1921, was a sharp change of economic direction, the New Economic Policy (NEP). Peasants were no longer to be required to give up all their produce beyond subsistence, but had to pay a fixed grain tax and could sell their surplus freely in the open market. By extension, retail trade in general was freed. Private entrepreneurs were permitted to run small plants, and even foreign capital was invited, without much success, to enter on the basis of concessions. Control of nationalized industries was relaxed and managers were instructed to try to make a profit. A new currency was introduced and stabilized. Civil, land, and criminal codes were introduced, largely copied from German models with secondary place for "revolutionary consciousness." The private sector of industry never employed over one-fifth of the industrial workers, but it quickly provided increasing quantities of the most necessary consumer goods. Russia seemed for a few years to be successfully evolving a mixed economy.

Many thought that this retreat meant the end of communism, but the Leninists had no intention of loosening the grip of the party. Instead, they stiffened its monopoly. To have granted any degree of freedom would have been to surrender power. The last non-Bolshevik leftist organizations and publications were eliminated, and the Kron-

stadt sailors who demanded fulfillment of the promises of the revolution were executed. The local soviets, which had lost most of their
autonomy during the civil conflict, were reduced to agencies of the
central government. The nominally independent Soviet nations, the
Ukraine, Georgia with the other Caucasian republics, and others were
amalgamated, 1922-23, into the nominally federal Union of Soviet
Socialist Republics.

Control within the party was strengthened. In March, 1919, the five-
member Politburo was formally established as a guiding nucleus of the
Central Committee. In 1921, meetings of the Central Committee were
reduced from twice monthly to once in two months, thereby effectively
removing this body from decision-making. The Tenth Party Congress,
March, 1921, was a watershed in the suppression of dissent. A minority,
expressing the workers' disillusionment, spoke for a greater role in
management of industry for the trade-unions, as representatives of the
proletariat which was to exercise its dictatorship. Another group, kin-
dred in spirit, pleaded for more democracy in party affairs and freedom for local party bodies. Lenin made some concessions, mostly of
form; but he pushed through a resolution sharply condemning the
deviation and another forbidding factionalism in general. Party members, although free to discuss undecided questions and to make proposals, were not to get together to promote them. The Tenth Congress
was followed by the first purge of the party. About a quarter of the
membership was stricken from the rolls, including some who had supported the Workers' Opposition. It was also becoming ordinary policy
to assign disapproved leaders to distant posts. The party bureaucracy
grew; a commission set up to check bureaucratic practices became another instrument of centralization. Local party organizations found
themselves turned into administrative agencies. At all levels, power
gravitated toward the center, from committees to secretaries, and especially to the Secretariat of the Central Committee, headed by Stalin
from 1922. The Cheka, set up to deal with counterrevolutionaries, received the power to arrest party members.

The Soviet Russian state inevitably continued much of the substance
of the tsarist state. The government which came out of the crucible of
the revolution and subsequent turmoil was strongly centralist; it was

executive-dominated, with no legislature or judiciary capable of checking the administrative powers. It was elitist, concentrating authority in the hands of a very few persons around an exalted leader. Criticism of Lenin became as inadmissible as of Nicholas or Alexander. It was assumed that a dictatorship—of the party standing for the proletariat—was the necessary form of government for Russia until the millennium or world revolution.

The overall effect of the Russian Revolution was to strengthen the state. If the middle and more independent sectors of society were weak before the revolution, afterwards they were practically nonexistent. There were few persons of education in Lenin's government except the returned exiles, who formed a thin cap on the cruder mass. The upheaval brought into positions of authority men from the more primitive layers of the population. Their mentality was premodern and uninfluenced by the West; in due course they became the basis of Stalin's power.

The Soviet synthesis, however, was to a large extent the work of Lenin. He was a remarkable blend of doer and thinker, extreme and dogmatic in ideas but flexible in means, a utopian always ready to compromise principles. He could be very hard. Belief in the necessity of force to bring change was an integral part of his political philosophy. He freely approved of executions of many persons—only marginally guilty—for moral effect. He once remarked to the writer Gorky, ". . . it is necessary to beat people on the head, beat them pitilessly, although our ideal is opposed to all coercion. . ."[1] Opposition to his views roused him to fury. However, he had some willingness to consult and listen to different viewpoints. In contrast to Stalin, he accepted opponents back into responsible positions when they repented. Lenin was a man of culture, influenced by Western values. He was much impressed with modern technology. The socialist society, he predicted, would be practically a technocracy, with politicians replaced by engineers and agronomists. Whatever his ambitions, they were not for personal adulation and luxury. He was always modest in his ways even as his associates were turning from idealistic abnegation to enjoyment of the fruits of power.

His better side came to the fore in his last months. In May, 1922, he suffered a stroke and remained more or less incapacitated until his death in January, 1924. Then he reflected on his life's works. Observing how the old bureaucratic tyranny was coming back under Soviet forms and slogans, he became concerned that his state fulfill more of its promise of liberation. He proposed that the powers of the central regime be limited to foreign affairs and defense. He came violently in conflict with Stalin over the latter's maltreatment of Georgia. Although he had found Stalin's political style acceptable during many years, Lenin in his political testament proposed that he be removed from the position of General Secretary and replaced by someone "more patient, more loyal, more polite and more attentive to comrades, less capricious, etc." As long as the Leninists were in charge, the Bolshevik regime was not prepared to realize the potentialities of despotism of de-westernized Russia. This was left to Stalin, whose ascension to dictatorship began as Lenin and those who had formed the Bolshevik party in exile began to lose their grip on Soviet affairs.

FOOTNOTES

1. Quoted by John Reshetar, *A Concise History of the Communist Party of the Soviet Union* (Praeger, New York, 1964), p. 143.

CHAPTER 4

Stalin's Russia

RISE OF STALIN

Joseph V. Stalin was born in 1879 in a small Caucasian town, son of a drunken cobbler. Far from the cultured upper-middle class milieu of the Ulianovs, Stalin's background was of ex-serfdom and deprivation. His illiterate mother had sufficient ambition for her only surviving child (whose father died when he was eleven) to send him to a seminary to prepare him for the priesthood. Like Lenin, young Stalin was a capable student; but he got into difficulties, was expelled from school, and entered the revolutionary movement. However, while Lenin went on to an émigré existence in such intellectual centers as London and Geneva, Stalin never left Georgia until age twenty-five, when the police sent him to Siberia, and he subsequently made only brief stays abroad.

Stalin, unlike most of the Leninist leadership, had a genuine class grievance against tsarist society. As seen in the violent language of his prerevolutionary writings, Stalin's hatred for the privileged was more like that of the anarchist sailors who in 1917 shot well-dressed men for sport. Unlike the exile politicians, he had little education, and he knew no Western language. His activity was illegal and by the code of the day criminal. Lenin's world merged into that of Western socialist philosophy, Stalin's into that of banditry. He was, for instance, involved in "expropriations." There has also been speculation that he may have been involved with the police; if he had such a skeleton in his closet, this might account for some of the paranoia he displayed when his power became absolute.

Although lacking in human warmth—his biography is practically silent about friendships—Stalin had organizational talent. He rose rapidly in the Caucasian revolutionary movement, won the confidence of Lenin, and was coopted into the Central Committee when Lenin wanted faithful adherents to staff the newly separated party. Not an outstanding agitator, Stalin played no conspicuous part in 1917, although an enormous effort was made in years of his absolutism to portray him as coleader of the revolution. His star began rising when organization of the new state became the Bolshevik task. He was fairly prominent in the civil war—perhaps then acquiring the overconfidence in his strategic abilities which proved disastrous in the Second World War.

As commissar of nationalities in the new government Stalin had charge of relations with a large part of the population. He was a member of the Politburo (or "Policy Bureau") of the Central Committee which became steadily more ascendant as the Central Committee itself became larger and met less often. There was also set up the Orgburo ("Organizational Bureau") to direct the party's organizational work; and after March, 1921, Stalin was the only person on these two leading party organs. He also found his way into about a dozen other party or state offices, and was the head of the Workers-Peasants' Inspectorate, with the authority to reward and especially to punish. In April, 1922, he acquired the office that was to be his power-base for thirty-one years when he was appointed General Secretary of the Central Committee, with two faithful adherents, Molotov and Kuibyshev, as deputies.

From this date, which nearly coincided with the incapacity of Lenin, Stalin was probably the most influential individual (after Lenin, so far as he could function) in the Soviet government. He had a strong contingent of supporters in the Central Committee and even more in the district and local party offices to which most of the top leaders paid little attention. The secretaryship gave Stalin an unequalled handle on power, to the potentialities of which his rivals were strangely oblivious. He kept the files and had most say-so about assigning cadres. In view of this, it is difficult to understand not that Stalin became dictator but that it took him so long. He did not rise conspicuously during Lenin's illness, but Lenin's injunction that Stalin be replaced as General Secretary only slightly weakened his position, as the testament was read only to a few leading Communists, and the Politburo was not prepared to heed it against a man who seemed loyally to carry out its will. Lenin's other prescription to check the ambitions of Stalin was surprisingly naive, to enlarge the Central Committee from twenty-seven to "fifty or a hundred" by adding good proletarians. Stalin carried this out to the detriment of the party intellectuals and to his own benefit.

Stalin rose primarily by use of the channels of the party organization, intrigue, and the building of a following, as a manipulating leader might anywhere. He had patience for routine work which outwardly more brilliant men avoided. He kept calm and spoke little and usually only to make practical proposals. He always acted in the name of Lenin's party, to which he professed perfect loyalty when it was rapidly becoming Stalin's party. Stalin also built up the cult of Lenin, whose cadaver was placed on permanent display in Red Square in the Russian tradition of reverence of saints whose remains miraculously resist decomposition. Lenin was made a symbol of superhuman authority, and Stalin presented himself as the best and truest disciple in apostolic succession.

After Stalin honored Lenin by enrolling many new proletarian members, nearly doubling the party, he brought about the expulsion of a large number of less reliable elements and had a party more amenable to his desires. He also appointed more men of working class background to party posts. Marxists could only applaud these measures, but they meant bringing in persons of mentality close to Stalin's. The devotees of world revolution were yielding to the homebred type, who saw Stalin as one of their own and who owed their advancement to him.

It was necessary that the leader have a claim to doctrinal authority, and Stalin published in 1924 a major work, *Foundations of Leninism*, emphasizing organization, unity, discipline, and the authority of the party. Shortly after this, he came upon the idea of "Socialism in One Country." This thesis that the Soviet regime and its progress toward socialism could go forward without assistance from world revolution or the laggard German proletariat had a powerful appeal for Communists weary of waiting. Basically a doctrine of Russia first, it reversed the original priorities and subordinated the universal to the Russian cause.

The idea of socialism in one country was most effective against Trotsky, high priest of the internationalist revolutionary cause and Stalin's rival in the civil war. Trotsky was a brilliant writer, a greater hero of the revolution and of the civil war than Stalin, and was commander of the armed forces. But he was arrogant and incapable of working well with anyone but subordinates, and something of an outsider among the old Bolsheviks, having joined only in 1917. The party leaders were much more afraid of him than of the less conspicuous Stalin. Stalin was hence able to join with Kamenev and Zinoviev—who led the attack—and to isolate Trotsky.

By 1925 Trotsky had been sufficiently weakened so that Stalin, who ever undermined his opponents by dividing them, could ally himself with the moderates in the party against Kamenev and Zinoviev. Against them Stalin used the unpopularity of their program of squeezing the peasants and forcing the pace of industrialization and their history of disagreements with Lenin. Stalin easily mobilized party majorities to condemn them in the name of party unity and the Leninist no-faction rule. The last important display of opposition within the party came at the Fourteenth Congress, in December, 1925, when Stalinists shouted down the Leningrad (formerly Petrograd) delegation, still faithful to Zinoviev.

In the fall of 1927, the oppositionists belatedly and futilely tried to rouse the people against the danger of a Stalinist-bureaucratic tyranny, as though they had believed in the rights of the people against the party. Trotsky was banished to Central Asia and later exiled, a mistake Stalin would not repeat. More oppositionists were expelled from the party. They might recant, but if they were allowed to come back degraded, it was only on sufferance of the boss, who in due course had them all executed. After 1927, it was no longer possible to contest party elections or to appeal to the party as a whole; dissenters were driven to illegal printing and the holding of forbidden meetings, as the last more or less independent organizations were banned. The party by now was enlarged to over a million members, and composed of, or at least led by, careerists who knew that their prosperity depended upon pleasing the Stalinists at the center.

In 1928-29, no longer having allies but only subordinates, Stalin turned on Bukharin and the other "moderates," who had recently helped him defeat the leftists. After 1930, only Stalinists remained in the Politburo, and even when Stalin's position was weakened by the sufferings of the people and mass unrest of the peasants, there was no concerted move against him. There were still some with sufficient independence of mind to oppose Stalin's excesses, especially in regard to the purges; these men were disposed of in the latter 1930's. But from 1929, Stalin was the new autocrat of all the Russias.

PLANNED INDUSTRIALIZATION

No sooner had Stalin done away with opposition within the party than he moved to transform Soviet society and economy through industrialization under party-state direction and the collectivization of the peasantry. The Soviet economy had done very well under the mixed regimen of Lenin's New Economic Policy, industrial production in 1928 having surpassed the prewar level. The unworkable controls imposed during the civil war were largely given up in the relaxation of the NEP, and the planning agency, Gosplan, tried to do little more than planning agencies in Western countries nowadays. But in 1928, Stalin called upon the planners to set targets for a five year period, inaugurating the series of five-year plans which continues to this day.

Then, in a grand campaign for storming the heights of production, targets were again and again raised to levels of fantasy, in the style of Mao's Great Leap Forward. In the excitement and revival of revolutionary spirit, the wildest expectations were created, as though the utopia which had not come from political action was to be brought by economic miracle. After a few years of hard work, Russia would be industrialized, modernized and rolling in abundance.

By great sacrifices, the bases of heavy industry, especially coal, iron, and steel, were greatly expanded in the First Five-Year Plan. The second, beginning in 1933, was less overambitious, better organized, and more successful. The first two plans raised the national product by perhaps 7-9% yearly—estimates vary according to weights and prices— from 1928-37. Rate of investment, perhaps the chief key to growth, was doubled to about a quarter of national income, near which level it has remained. Not least, the plans gave the Soviet Union the foundations of an armaments industry to carry it through the Second World War.

But lack of experience and inefficient mechanisms of planning and control caused enormous confusion and waste. Costly imported machines rusted or were wrecked by ignorant peasants drawn into factories. Factories were built in the wrong places, supplies were uncoordinated, etc. While the five-year plan was building up heavy industry, it destroyed much consumer goods industry and artisan production. Consumer goods production and the standard of living fell sharply until 1934. The 1928 level of workers' real incomes was not re-attained until 1952.

The economic drive gave a potent stimulus to education. Soviet education had been rather loose and general, with slack discipline. Stalin turned it to purposeful study, and Soviet institutes began turning out a rapidly growing number of technicians. Stalinist Russia became the first country to put education purposefully at the service of economic growth and national strength.

The new engineers and managers rose rapidly in the maturing industrial society. Stalin, by 1931, was branding equalitarianism as deviationist and petty-bourgeois, and wage differentials in industry rose from about 1:3 in 1928 to 1:40 in 1940, while the high elite was coming into royal luxuries far from the austerity of the early Bolsheviks. Stalinist industrialization also required discipline of labor. After 1930 internal passports were introduced, rations and living space were taken from those who quit their jobs, and controls and penalties were multiplied until in 1940 workers were strictly frozen to their jobs. The trade-unions were also turned practically into agencies of the state, whose chief function was cooperation in the fulfillment of the plan.

By compulsion, incentives, and persuasion Stalin thus engineered a westernization of Russia like that of Peter but far more drastic. Its basic purpose was the same, to secure the strength of Russia. The backwardness of Russian industry, especially heavy, had been a major factor of defeat in the First World War; and Russia was relatively farther behind in 1928 than it had been in 1913. The drive for rapid industrialization was also rationalized on the basis that heavy industry would make it possible subsequently to produce the abundance of consumer goods prerequisite for the Communist society. But consumer goods production remained the stepchild of planning.

Political motives also figured. The Bolsheviks envisioned ruling an industrial, not an agrarian, society. They were still extremely weak in the countryside, and have always been more successful in the management of industry than agriculture. The country had recovered sufficiently by 1928 that a more ideological-political approach seemed possible; the retreat to limited private enterprise under the NEP was a regrettable concession to be undone when conditions permitted. The methods used were dictated less by the desire for rapid economic growth than by Stalin's modes of political action. The plans themselves hardly amounted to economic efforts to coordinate production; they were rather vehicles of political mobilization and centralization.

COLLECTIVIZATION

The storm of industrialization in the cities was mild compared to the tempest of collectivization which struck the villages at the same time. The peasants were hit by the most massive transformation ever inflicted on Russia. Millions were driven from their homes and deported or deprived of grain stocks and left to starve. Those who remained had to farm largely for the grain collectors, and there was little amelioration until after the death of Stalin.

The rationalization of collectivization was economic; it was necessary for the state to secure more grain to feed the growing cities and to export in order to purchase equipment for the five-year plan. Stalin argued, misusing statistics, that peasants were withholding grain from the market. Brushing aside the argument of Bukharin and the "rightists" in the party that the peasants should be given incentives to produce more, he contended that it was indispensable to get the peasants into collectives where their produce would be subject to control and removal.

The argument was made in ideological terms, but Marx and Engels had not tried to decide the future of agriculture and Lenin before the revolution apparently had not proposed collectivization. The "ideological" demand for collectivization covered a political demand. The independent peasants, particularly those who had risen to a modest prosperity in the years of some economic freedom, represented the chief noncommunist force in the country, and the Soviet state could not feel secure as long as the peasant majority was independent of it. The prosperous peasantry also formed the principal backing for the last important non-Stalinist sector of the party, the "rightists" or moderates, whose most effective spokesman was Bukharin, a few years earlier leader of the ultra-left. When Stalin got the better of the "rightists" at the top of the party, he turned to liquidating their source of support.

In November, 1929, Stalin spoke of the "year of the great change" and called for a rapid speedup in the establishment of collective and state farms, which the party had promoted half-heartedly since the revolution. He proceeded with the same violence and haste which he had applied to industrialization. Peasants were bludgeoned into full collectives wherein they had to surrender not only their landholdings but equipment, draft animals, and for a time even their chickens. By dint of veritable warfare, well over half of peasant households were thus collectivized, at least on paper, by March, 1930. This was coupled with a violent campaign against the church. But excesses of stupidity and cruelty so embittered the peasants that the authority of the regime became questionable in many places. Stalin called a halt, blamed overzealous subordinates, decried attacks on the church, and said that collective farms should permit households the use of a small plot of land and the possession of a limited amount of livestock. He also proclaimed the freedom of peasants to leave the newly created collectives, and most of those who had nominally joined promptly did so, although this meant leaving behind their tools and livestock. But the campaign was soon resumed with more judicious use of force and better effect. By the middle of the following year, the majority of Russia's peasants were collective farmers, and by 1934 collectivization was basically complete.

All who might be assumed to be against collectivization were removed. Consequently, the collectivization campaign ran into "the liquidation of the kulaks as a class." In the old Russian village, "kulaks," or wealthier peasants, apt to be money-lenders, were regarded as grasping and exploitative. Now millions of better-off peasants were attacked as "kulak" wreckers and class enemies and ruthlessly deported. Probably well over five million died from harsh treatment and in the famine brought about by seizure of grain stocks.

After 1934, the peasants gradually became resigned to their new condition, wherein they were required to work for the collective which turned over most of its production to the state; but there was a heritage of alienation that could fade only with the rise of a new generation. Half of Russia's livestock was lost; for about five years, production was much reduced and thereafter it rose quite slowly. Collectivization was an economic calamity of the first magnitude, despite and not because of which industrialization proceeded. It was, however, a political victory, and it continues to be celebrated as one of Stalin's achievements. It gathered the peasants into an organization commanded by a party-chosen man, where the results of their labor were subject to expropriation. It made the countryside more governable in the Soviet manner, while creating hundreds of thousands of controlling positions in party and state apparatuses. The Nazis occupying Russian territories recognized the utility of the collectives, to which they were ideologically opposed, for grain collection and political control.

THE PURGES

Stalin's third great measure for the remaking of Soviet society was the purge, cleansing the population of political independence. No more than planned industrialization and collectivization, however, was terrorism Stalin's invention. It began practically with the revolution and it has outlived Stalin.

Under Lenin, the idea of murdering comrades for differences of personal affiliation would have seemed madness. However, Lenin set a precedent in a show trial of Socialist-Revolutionaries sentenced to death in 1922. Reprisals against errant Bolsheviks grew after opposition from other parties was eliminated and the political struggle, so far as it continued, became factionalism within the party; and gradually sterner measures were taken to enforce discipline. From 1928 there were more show trials for alleged espionage and counterrevolutionary activities. During the First Five-Year Plan, two to three thousand direly needed engineers and specialists were arrested for alleged wrecking and sabotage and put to manual labor. The liquidation of the kulaks strengthened the habit of using force for political ends and began the mass employment of forced labor. It also evoked an enlarged police organization given to coercion and the exploitation of prisoners.

The Great Terror began with the assassination of Sergei Kirov in December, 1934. A relatively popular and intelligent Stalinist, Kirov may have posed some threat to Stalin's monopoly of power. He was shot under circumstances indicating complicity of Stalinists if not of Stalin. But his murder was held up as a frightful example of the cost of slackness toward the enemy, and hundreds of persons unconnected with the assassination were massacred and thousands were arrested and sentenced to forced labor.[1]

The purge rolled on through 1935 but rose to full fury in 1936. In August, Kamenev, Zinoviev, and fourteen associates were publicly charged with organizing, in complicity with arch-villain Trotsky, a terrorist gang. To the amazement of the world, they publicly confessed. Hundreds of thousands followed them to prison or to the grave. Another great show trial of ex-oppositionists was held in January, 1937. In March some three thousand of the secret police were executed. In June the armed forces were hit; leading generals and then officers of lower ranks were struck down. In March, 1938, another group of prominent Bolsheviks, including Bukharin, several other ex-members of the Politburo, and Yagoda, head of the police until September, 1936, had their turn at the dock, to tell the world how they had been secret enemies of the Soviet state and hirelings of capitalist powers.

The trials were only the publicized aspect of the slaughter which flooded across the Soviet land from the summer of 1936 until the summer of 1938, hitting every sphere of Soviet life. The more responsible a person's position, the poorer his chances of escaping, except for Stalin's immediate coterie. About half of the membership of the party was removed. Nearest to immune were members of the tsarist intelligentsia and churchmen, persons of no possible political potential. Worst struck were generals and party bosses. Of 121 regional first secretaries, only Khrushchev, Zhdanov and Beria escaped. Stalin spared no fellow members of the six persons named by Lenin's testament as the most important in the party, of the seven members of the Politburo of 1924, or of Lenin's fifteen-man government. Of 1966 delegates to the "Congress of Victors" of 1934, 1108 were shot; only thirty-five returned to the March, 1939, congress. About half the officer corps of the army was shot, the percentage increasing to nearly 100% at the top; only those who had been with Stalin in the civil war had good chances of escaping. Many in the police forces were taken, too. Provocateurs whose confessions were used to lend plausibility to show trials were subject to execution.

Old Bolsheviks of the intelligentsia were nearly wiped out except for a few women. Layers of management were removed, replaced, and the replacements taken in turn, even three or four times. Leaders in minority regions were suspect; of 102 members and candidates of the Ukrainian Central Committee three survived, and other Soviet republics fared similarly. Persons with any foreign connection, even stamp collectors and those who chanced to receive a letter from abroad, were in gravest danger. Many foreign Communists were liquidated, particularly members of the once-potent German party who had found refuge from Hitlerism. The leadership of the Polish party was obliterated, and others fared nearly as badly. In sum, about thirteen million lives were taken by execution and hardships of labor camps. A large majority of sentences were not execution but forced labor in intemperate regions, on construction, mining, lumbering, or other projects; about eight million were so engaged in 1938. Only 5-10% ever regained freedom.

Cheap labor was undoubtedly one reason for the magnitude of the purges, but one can search in vain for a rational explanation. There was no excuse of crisis or danger; the damage inflicted on the army reflects indifference to needs of defense. If the Nazis had struck in 1939, they would have encountered a crippled Red Army, the reconstruction of which really began only after the war with Finland. There was no social purpose, such as that which supposedly justified the liquidation of the kulaks. There was no rationale in Marxist ideology.

In part, the extensiveness of the purges was due to bureaucratic stupidity made possible by indifference to human values, allowing the police organization, the NKVD, to build its empire. Obtaining of the confessions on which trials depended had a snowball effect as one accused ordinarily implicated more. One purpose was to find scapegoats for the failures of agriculture and industry. All manner of faults were ascribed to "wrecking," from industrial accidents and production of shoddy goods to the prevalence of weeds in the fields and ticks on cows. This may have been fairly successful, as people were prone to believe that the supreme ruler could not be at fault. The primary motive, however, seems to have been the desire to extirpate every vestige of opposition. Stalin was inordinately suspicious and apparently felt insecure in his illegitimate power, constrained to keep struggling against enemies in order to stay on top. Such opposition as existed was scattered, without a program, without even a coherent will to resist destruction; but Stalin may have believed there were indeed plots against him. His answer was to pound out of the Russian people for many years any willfulness or independent spirit and to make them, high and low, passive and servile.

MATURE STALINISM

As Lenin moved beyond Marx, Stalin went beyond Lenin in stressing political power and conformity. He destroyed not only competing parties but all independent forces in the land. Industry and agriculture were placed under centralized control so far as mechanically feasible.

Labor was strictly regimented and trade-unions were, like the party and soviets, turned into "transmission belts," as Stalin expressed it. Art, literature, and music were harnessed; artists were no longer told what they might not do but were instructed what they must do for the party and the leader. For example, Stalin had some 200 plays written to glorify the Moscow-Volga Canal. The schools were made authoritarian agencies of indoctrination and the imparting of useful skills. Soviet philosophy, economics, and history were purged of independent thinking; there was to be a single way and a single truth dictated from on high. Stalin nullified the modest autonomy enjoyed by the legally sovereign Soviet republics and centralized the Russian realm as never before; the Georgian was the prince of russifiers. The church was cowed and religion was crushed to insignificance. There was no politics in the ordinary sense but only a covert struggle of individuals or at most cliques for influence with higher powers.

When Stalin had achieved this condition, it remained not to change but to rule. Stalin brought to an end the revolutionary mentality and, despite formal adherence to Marxism-Leninism, made the Soviet Union a basically conservative state. There was a return to Russian patriotism and nationalism, and old tsars were restored to respectability. Privileged groups were created, whose interests lay not with the masses but with the rulers. Not only were ranks restored in the army but officers were instructed in dancing and etiquette. Revolutionary Russia found the family backward; Stalinist Russia turned back to it as keeper of order. Divorce was made difficult and abortion illegal; mothers were rewarded for numerous children; a new puritanism covered public behavior. The bureaucratized autocracy of Stalin reverted to the sixteenth century Muscovite despotism of ruler and slaves rather than the relatively relaxed autocracy of the last tsarist generation. Stalin was often and rightly called a Red Tsar. He regarded himself as successor of Peter and especially of Ivan the Terrible. He was practically deified as the embodiment of truth and power, symbol of the union of the peoples. His pronouncements were close to god-given truth not only on political and economic affairs but on history, linguistics, or genetics; his thought and person were supposed to be the inspiration of those blessed by his leadership.

Stalin's mystique was furthered by aloofness; Muscovites might only glimpse his curtained black limousine speeding along guarded roads. Secrecy became the rule. In the 1920's, the Soviet Union published an enormous amount of economic and other data, but this was cut down in the 1930's to practically no solid information. The present was gilded; the past was shrouded and remade, with events and persons inconvenient to the leader obliterated while his own image was haloed. Behind the screen, power flowed in Byzantine channels. The police, the party apparatus, to a lesser extent the military, the regular bureaucracy and economic managers, exerted obscure influence. Power gravitated to the secretariat of the General Secretary, composed of men totally invisible to the public. In the fear of deviant ideas and distrust for all that could not be controlled, Stalinist Russia isolated itself from the outside world. Except for a few carefully screened officials, it became impossible for Soviet citizens to pass the borders. Information of the outside world was rigorously excluded. Foreign trade was discouraged and greatly reduced after an early surge of imports for industrialization.

Stalinism had obvious points of resemblance to another modern despotism, that of Hitler's Germany, for which it was for a time verbal antagonist, then half-ally, and finally deadly enemy. Both made the select but mass party a main political instrument, and coupled the party with an ideology more revolutionary in pretense than in reality. Although the Nazis glorified force more and had a more military ethos, the difference was one of degree. The NKVD had something in common with the Gestapo, although the sweep of the former was much broader; in Nazi Germany, insiders were nearly immune, while in Stalin's Russia they were in the greatest danger. Adulation of the leader was more pervasive in the Soviet Union, although it conflicted with the spirit of Marxism-Leninism, while the "Führerprinzip" was the heart of Nazi ideology. Planning of the economy was much more effective in the Soviet Union, as was the mobilization of literature and art, but Nazi Germany followed some of the same patterns. Anti-Semitism came to the fore in Stalinism only after the war and was never explicit. There seems to have been mutual influence. The Nazi flag, party organization, and methods of propaganda and control were influenced by Bolshevik originals. Stalin, on the other hand, reverted to Russian nationalism as the Nazi success in the exploitation of German nationalism was becoming apparent. He embarked on the purges of the party just a few months after Hitler's successful blood purge in June, 1934.

However, Stalinism, unlike Nazism, had its mission of modernization and industrialization. Industrialization requires subordination, specialization, and bureaucracy, as well as education; and it can be advanced by governmental action. Stalinism presented itself as a remedy for Russian backwardness. Collectivization shook up the countryside; forced-draft industrialization might be considered necessary to initiate rapid progress in backward Russia. Stalinism can also be understood as a populist despotism suitable for an age when modern communications make it possible to reach all the people and bring them into the framework of the state. About the time of his advance to the heights of despotic power, Stalin introduced impressive democratic reforms. The superficially democratic constitution of 1936 provided for direct elections by equal, secret ballot to all soviets, from top to bottom, and gave these ample paper powers. Stalin also introduced secret balloting into the party elections which are less unimportant than the soviet elections. Most of all, he satisfied aspirations of the masses by opening all careers to the talented, making peasants' sons and serfs' grandsons into engineers and managers, if not commissars and party bosses.

The steady advance of the Soviet system to the absolutism of full Stalinism makes the process seem inevitable. It is unlikely that Stalin in 1922 had any idea of the road ahead. But wherever he could overcome resistance, he moved ruthlessly further, until he had removed everyone conceivably inconvenient to himself.

Stalin was able to do this despite lack of personal charm or charisma. He was a dull speaker and writer, repetitious and given to clichés, although he could state neo-Marxist positions effectively. No one ever credited him with the ability to hypnotize an audience or to dominate those with whom he spoke as Hitler could. Nor did he demonstrate any great understanding of the economic and political needs of his country. His victory was entirely of the organization, won through manipulation and management of men.

SETTLED DICTATORSHIP

With the end of the mass purges in 1939, the Soviet Union entered its postrevolutionary period, and the following thirty-odd years brought less change than the previous decade. The people and the ruling apparatus have become far more educated and sophisticated, and controls have become more regularized. But the apparatus of party and state, without overt opposition and only slight indications of political differences, runs in the tracks on which Stalin set it.

The machinery of control of the economy has been little changed. Five-Year plans, as inaugurated by Stalin, go on. The collective farm statute of 1935 underwent only minor modification in 1969, although the farms are physically much changed. The constitution adopted in 1936 remains with insignificant amendment. The controls Stalin established over literature and the arts function with marginal relaxation; the official doctrine is still Socialist Realism. The replacement of personal dictatorship by more or less collective leadership has brought less change than was to be expected.

Terror continued after 1939, but it was quiet and took few of the top leadership, which remained stable until after Stalin's death. There was likewise little change in policies. But military budgets began climbing after Hitler made evident in 1934 his disinterest in continuing the old German friendship with the Soviet Union and especially after he began in 1936 to play up anticommunism as an international cause. Attention was now directed outward; and negotiations were carried on in the spirit of power politics, first with the Western powers and then more successfully with Germany. By the agreement of August 23, 1939, the Soviet Union recovered most of the territories lost in the aftermath of the revolution. These were sovietized in 1940 and added to the Soviet Union as four new republics, the former Baltic states, and Moldavia (Bessarabia).

Accustomed to infallibility, Stalin ignored numerous warnings of the German attack. The assault of June 22, 1941, seems to have dazed him; he kept silent for eleven days. The Soviet forces at the beginning of the war were, despite large expenditures, badly equipped and incompetently led. The early defeats would have liquidated a country with less manpower and less space to sacrifice. But an extremely stringent mobilization of manpower and resources was put into effect. Soviet munitions production rose rapidly to a level comparable with that of the United States despite the much smaller industrial base. The war showed how effective a tightly organized, disciplined system could be when motivated by strong popular emotions.

Stalin does not seem to have been a good war leader. He visited the front only once and briefly. He must bear much responsibility not only for unreadiness in 1941 but for tremendous losses through encirclement of armies which he refused to allow to retreat. But it was his merit to bring out the patriotism of the Russian people. He stepped down to address them in human terms as "Comrades, citizens, brothers and sisters," appealing to the instincts of a threatened people. Ideological censorship was largely forgotten, and many inspiring patriotic works were produced. The government came to an understanding with the church, which in return strongly supported the war effort. Controls over the collective farms were relaxed and peasants were encouraged to produce however they could; although most of their manpower was taken away, they did so quite effectively. The doors of the party were opened to good fighters for the fatherland with little regard for ideological conformity. Old national themes stirred the people; even Pan-Slavism, the imperial Russian ideal of brotherhood of Slavic peoples, was called upon to replace proletarian internationalism.

But as soon as victory was assured, there began a return to the ideological-party approach and a reassertion of discipline. Soviet spokesmen began warning again of the dangers of "capitalist encirclement." The image of the world was redrawn in ideological terms, and repressions of deviants were resumed. The Soviet Union continued to concentrate on military-industrial muscle. With the intensification of the cold war in 1947, a deeper chill descended. Writers, artists, even musicians, were called upon to recant; only totally conformist works extolling the Soviet system, its glories and its leader, were permitted. Xenophobia was pushed to new heights, with insistence on Soviet and Russian superiority in all things. Most useful inventions were found to have been made by Russians but stolen by the West. The extreme was reached in 1949, when the Soviet Union saw only satellites and unconditional adherents as friends, the economy was being remilitarized, and a purge, striking some two thousand functionaries, silently hit Leningrad. In December the deification of the leader reached its zenith in the celebrations of his seventieth birthday. *Pravda* was still publishing congratulations two and a half years later.

In the last years of Stalin's life, the Soviet Union was showing signs of change. Although Stalin seems to have opposed any detente with the West, there were moves toward opening up foreign trade, which had shrunk to a trickle, outside the bloc. The Nineteenth Congress of the Party was called in the fall of 1952, although Stalin did not like large gatherings, even of handpicked supporters, and there had been no congress since 1939. Stalin, whose mental powers were declining, seems to have felt his authority slipping. There were a series of grim purge trials in Eastern Europe, and in 1952 Stalin's native Georgia was hard hit. According to Khrushchev's Secret Speech, Stalin no longer felt able to work with the twelve-man Politburo but used ad hoc committees. At the Nineteenth Congress he enlarged the Politburo to a twenty-five man Presidium of the Central Committee, presumably because of distrust of the old oligarchs.

From the beginning of 1953, the Soviet press was calling for vigilance against enemy agents and wreckers. A number of Kremlin doctors, mostly Jewish, were arrested and accused of medical murder and of plotting, with Zionist organizations and the American intelligence service, against leading Soviet generals. The aging Stalin may have wished to restore full autocracy by a shakeup like Mao's Cultural Revolution of 1966. In an atmosphere of mounting apprehension, March 5, 1953, the dictator died.

FOOTNOTES

1. For a full account of the purges see Robert Conquest, *The Great Terror* (Macmillan Co., New York, 1968).

CHAPTER 5

New Directions

THE SUCCESSION

Stalin had prepared no succession, and no rule decreed how power should be transferred. His heirs themselves seem to have had little confidence in the stability of the regime, as they warned the people against "disorder and panic." But the party leadership carried on much as it had after Lenin's demise. There was not even an open political contest as occurred in the 1920's, with participation of a large number of party people. The struggle for predominance after Stalin was entirely among Stalinists whose political outlook had been almost indistinguishable, and it went on entirely in the shadows.

As after Lenin's death, there was established a collective leadership. For a brief time it seemed that Georgy Malenkov, apparently closest to Stalin, was moving into his place, as he was both party secretary and premier. But his colleagues forced him out of his position on the Secretariat, which was his chief source of power. The new regime spoke of return to Leninist principles and decried the harmfulness of one-man decisions; they dissociated themselves from the worst of Stalinism and courted popularity by acts of mercy and moderation. Criminal but not political prisoners were amnestied. The atmosphere of terror was lifted; Beria, Stalin's police chief, spoke of the need for socialist legality. There was a little opening to the outside world, and emphasis was slightly shifted to consumer goods.

Although out of the Secretariat, Malenkov remained the most prominent personality. Beside him stood the sinister Lavrenty Beria, whose cooperation was necessary in the organization of the regime. Nikita Khrushchev, like Stalin at an early stage, was more powerful than he appeared. He had spent a long time away from the center in the Ukraine, and his provincial experience probably gave him a better feeling for the needs of the country than those who knew only the recesses of the Kremlin. In September, 1953, he was made First Secretary, and he proceeded to make the party his power instrument. The others of the old inner circle, Molotov, Mikoyan, and Kaganovich, could hardly aspire to the top post.

The first break in the collective leadership was the ouster of Beria from control of the police in June and his execution in December. In the old style, he was accused of having been a longtime spy for the British, and a number of aides accompanied him in death. Leaders have not subsequently been so branded or physically liquidated.

Malenkov inaugurated something of a detente in international relations. By advocating developing light industry as rapidly as heavy, of, for instance, using aluminum for pans instead of airplanes, he aroused great expectations for improvement of the standard of living. To relieve overcentralization, he began to transfer thousands of plants to the jurisdiction of the separate republics. There was a thaw in literature and a beginning was made in the rehabilitation of purge victims. This tendency was apparently alarming to party stalwarts and the military-industrial complex, whose spokesman Khrushchev made himself. Toward the end of 1954, the Soviet Union saw the first public semidebate for twenty years: *Pravda* decried and *Izvestia* defended the lowered priority for heavy and defense industry. In February, 1955, Malenkov resigned as premier, although he stayed on the Presidium. The new head of administration was an ineffectual political soldier, Marshal Bulganin. For a few years there was an ostensible duumvirate of Khrushchev and Bulganin as heads of party and state apparatus, but the real power was clearly with the former.

Having associated himself with the military and reactionary wing in the ouster of Malenkov, Khrushchev proceeded in 1955 to follow the moderate course laid out by his predecessor. International detente and broadening of horizons were the keynote. The armed forces were reduced, and several steps were taken to improve relations with the outside world. Most remarkably, Khrushchev went to Belgrade to apologize to Tito, whom Stalin had excommunicated and anathematized eight years before. He also undertook a series of ideological revisions to rationalize and modernize the official Soviet outlook. In the nuclear age, war was no longer to be considered inevitable, as Lenin had insisted, but "peaceful coexistence" must be accepted as normal. Socialism then could come not only by violent revolution but by peaceful development and by different roads in different countries. The struggle of capitalism versus socialism was to be turned into a peaceful competition, which the Soviet Union was sure to win by economic and cultural superiority.

The softening of ideology was painful to many of the old Stalinists. But the connotations of peaceful coexistence were nothing compared to the effects of Khrushchev's denouncing Stalin as incompetent and a criminal at the February, 1956, Twentieth Congress of the Party. In his speech, delivered behind closed doors and read to party members throughout the Soviet Union, he charged Stalin with inordinate vanity and self-glorification, with murdering good Communists, and with abuse of power in the latter years of his rule. Much of the Stalin cult having rested on the image of the genius commander, Khrushchev portrayed Stalin as a military nincompoop. Khrushchev's purpose must have been in part to cast off burdens of the past and to promote a moral revival in the party. He was also attacking, by criticizing Stalin, his own chief contenders for power, Molotov, Malenkov, and associates, who had stood nearer to Stalin, while dissociating himself from the excesses of Stalinism.

De-Stalinization had effects, however, which Khrushchev had not foreseen. The peoples of the Soviet Union remained passive, but Eastern Europeans saw the dethronement of Stalin as a promise of freedom. There was a near-revolt in Poland, and a nationalistic uprising in Hungary could be suppressed only by Soviet forces. This threat to Russian dominion of Eastern Europe armed the opposition to Khrushchev, but it became strong enough to threaten him only after he pushed through an economic decentralization plan in May, 1957. This proposal for the dissolution of ministries in Moscow and transfer of staffs to provincial centers made economic sense, but for many bureaucrats being sent out of Moscow was banishment. The anti-Khrushchevites found themselves, in June, in an overwhelming majority on the Presidium, and only two members stood consistently by Khrushchev. His remedy was a constitutional innovation, an appeal to the Central Committee. Thanks to his having built up a personal following in the provinces, the Central Committee sustained Khrushchev and expelled his chief antagonists from the Presidium. But they were accused only of personal faults, not ideological sins as in past purges.

With this, Khrushchev had completed a rise to power distantly parallel to that of Stalin thirty years earlier. But he had no possibility of emulating the great dictator. He was much older—fifty-nine—when he became First Secretary, compared to Stalin's forty-three at accession to General Secretary. Although ruthless, Khrushchev does not seem to have desired bloodshed, and he was probably never strong enough to terrorize the party. There was no social transformation to justify mass repressions, or strong revolutionary-ideological feeling to give them a moral basis. Finally, the fact that the Soviet Union had matured into a modern industrial power with a fairly high educational level impeded, though it probably did not preclude, a Stalinesque dictatorship.

THE KHRUSHCHEV ALTERNATIVE

In his earlier career, Khrushchev had been more Stalinist than Stalin, and no one was louder in praise of the boss. However, he had a lively intelligence, was willing to try new departures, and aroused unaccustomed hopes of change. A contradictory character, he was basically ignorant but shrewd. With no liking for intellectuals, he yet permitted them some latitude. He talked of peace and made moves for relaxation, but he indulged in military threats far more than Stalin. He ended political terror and applied the death penalty for economic crimes. He was a party manipulator, but he actually sought popularity. He showed no definite principles and few scruples, but he seems to have genuinely desired the improvement of Soviet society.

Khrushchev proposed to return to the ideals of Leninism and the revolution. This meant reviving the party, which had decayed under Stalin because the boss leaned on various agencies to maximize his own power. Khrushchev increased the party role, especially its responsibility for industry and agriculture. He also sought to revive its political life. Unlike Stalin, Khrushchev liked party congresses and summoned them in 1956, 1959, and 1961. They did not again become real forums of controversy as in Lenin's time, and votes were always unanimous, as under Stalin; but they heard some interesting speeches, particularly from Khrushchev himself. The Central Committee, which had almost lapsed under Stalin, also had frequent and at times lively meetings. To shake up the local bosses Khrushchev instituted a plan for rotation of positions and limitation of length of service in one office. Khrushchev tried to be a better Marxist than Stalin. He lessened emphasis upon nationalistic and Russian themes, stepped up antireligious propaganda, cut down gross inequalities of income, and made some effort to equalize educational opportunities, requiring most students to spend two years at labor to become eligible for higher education. He nourished a Marxist vision of urbanizing the country, with ex-peasants living in apartment houses and busing to work.

Khrushchev attempted to reinstitute the goal of an eventual utopian-communist society, in which money should disappear because goods would be so abundant as to be freely apportioned to all according to need, and the state should wither away to leave the citizens to govern themselves. Many expected such a paradise on the morrow of the revolution, although it is not clear how seriously Lenin and other leading Bolsheviks took such dreams. They were partially put into effect in conditions of extreme lack of goods in the civil war; at least, money almost fell into disuse. For the rest, the civil war and then the needs of reconstruction justified indefinite postponement and Stalin discouraged the whole idea. Khrushchev's revised program of the party (the first revision since 1919), promulgated by the 1961 Twenty-Second Party Congress, mapped out the road to a partial communistic society to be established by 1980, with many more nonpaid services for the population and transfer of some state functions to "social" organizations of various kinds, without lessening the role of the party. For the moment, progress toward communism meant little more than such measures as expanding boarding schools and calling on volunteer police and irregular "comrade" courts to assist in law enforcement.

Such measures for "social control" suggested that communism might be a little like a beehive, as Khrushchev once put it. However, he recognized the need for change and innovation which the party could not always anticipate and was prepared to accept some loosening of controls. The latitude granted to dissent widened and narrowed from time to time, but areas of freedom were broadened to an extent inconceivable in Stalin's latter years. Foreign trade expanded, and many cultural exchanges were instituted with Western and other countries. Growing numbers of tourists were admitted. A street map of Moscow was put on sale in 1962; that was also the year a telephone directory was published for the first (and last) time. Russians lost their fear of contact with foreigners and a few were even permitted to travel abroad. Khrushchev received many foreign visitors and conversed with them with an ease and openness that was to become a fading memory after he left office. The production of consumer goods increased, although the traditional priority on heavy industry was retained. Such frivolities as lipstick became commonplace, and the Soviet Union began holding fashion shows.

Some literature very critical of Soviet faults, at least of the recent past, was published—accounts of concentration camp experiences and descriptions of life in the countryside. In 1961-62 the liberals were able to gain ascendancy in the Union of Writers. Khrushchev upbraided creative artists, even obscenely, but he did not have them arrested, and sometimes admitted that the writers were better judges of literature than the party. Scientists earned some immunity from party interference. Some discussion of international affairs was opened up, and scholars were permitted to treat the world as more complicated and shaded than the conventional class-struggle view.

Legal procedures were regularized (except for the popular justice mentioned), and more attention was given to the rights of the accused. Victims of Stalin's repressions were freed and rehabilitated, although the condemnations of such men as Trotsky, Kamenev, Zinoviev, Bukharin, and their fellows were not retracted. A little latitude of discussion was permitted within the party. To secure support for his policies, Khrushchev went outside the party elite, licensing rather wide-ranging debates of such matters as economic decentralization and educational reforms. Such debates were initiated by the top leadership and the conclusions were dictated by it, but it was an innovation that any controversy was let come to the surface. Khrushchev made a bow to the popular will by proclaiming that the "dictatorship of the proletariat" had after four decades ripened into the "state of the whole people."

Khrushchev gave more attention to agriculture, the weakest and most neglected sector of the economy. Here he came up with one panacea after another: the plowing of millions of acres of "Virgin Lands" of marginal rainfall in Kazakhstan, the planting of corn almost everywhere, the cultivation of grasslands, the "chemicalization" of agriculture. Most of all, however, he was disposed to reorganize. Economic planning was repeatedly shifted, divided, and rejoined in a confusion of state committees and councils. Rural administration was reorganized at least five times. Most drastic and most damaging was the move in 1962 to split the party and soviet system up to the provincial (oblast) level into agricultural and industrial sectors so that the party could give full attention to each. After all the panaceas, agriculture met such disaster in 1963 that the country was saved from hunger only by massive grain imports.

De-Stalinization was the key issue of Khrushchev's reign. To favor de-Stalinization was to favor freedom for literature and art, international contacts and detente, economic reform and consumerism; to oppose it was to stand for hard-fisted party rule. In this cleavage, Khrushchev could not take a firm stand. At the 1956 Congress he spoke only confidentially, curiously seeking to keep such a sensational matter within the elite. Moreover, his story was far from complete. Only the murder of good Stalinists was lamented. Not only did he not criticize collectivization, he failed to utter a word against the brutality with which it was carried through. In following years, rehabilitations proceeded irregularly and cautiously, and Stalin was praised off and on. The climax of de-Stalinization came only with the 1961 Congress, when Khrushchev coupled a new assault on Stalin with a renewed attack on Malenkov, Molotov, and company. Then, in published speeches, he sharpened his charges of criminality, including an implication of Stalin's complicity in the murder of Kirov that served as trigger for the purges. Stalin's body was removed from its place next to Lenin. In 1961-2, hundreds of Soviet cities, factories, collective farms, and the like lost the name of Stalin; hundreds of thousands of empty pedestals and a flurry of anti-Stalin writing brought de-Stalinization home to the Soviet people.

De-Stalinization facilitated ideological renewal, just as it hastened the rise to top rank of a new set of leaders, more or less beholden to Khrushchev. It pleased army commanders mindful of the damage and dishonor done to the armed forces by the purges. It was popular in the country at large, not least among millions of victims and their relatives. To the liberally inclined intellectuals, it was an unexpected boon.

But if de-Stalinization was helpful in the short run to Khrushchev, in the long run it was harmful to his authority. There was always resistance to it in the party. Many ordinary citizens, conditioned by long years of indoctrination, felt that Stalin was slandered, especially in his war role. And criticism of Stalin logically implicated the present leaders, all of whom had been close to him. Khrushchev claimed that he had opposed Stalin on occasion, but he thereby sanctioned opposition to himself. The defamation of such leaders as Molotov and Malenkov further undermined Soviet legitimacy. If de-Stalinization helped Khrushchev against the old guard who stood closer than he to Stalin, it left him defenseless against the younger men coming up.

The party stalwarts also saw Khrushchev threatening their authority by going outside the inner circle. He reached out to base himself, in part at least, on the specialists and administrators in various branches, frequently bringing in a corps of outsiders, officials, journalists, or sundry experts, to speak in favor of his ideas before the Central Committee. He used discussions in the press to advance measures, like educational reform, which the insiders viewed with displeasure. The conservatives found his impulsiveness and openness to novelty distasteful and dangerous to the comfortable status quo. The infection of Western decadence seemed to grow menacingly, as the street corners and cafes of Moscow and Leningrad were overrun with supermodern youth aping the latest styles of England and America.

Consequently, after 1961 Khrushchev's troubles piled up. He had difficulty in implementing economic reforms and in March, 1962, he seems to have failed to secure approval of his consumer goods program. His proposal to raise his son-in-law, Adzhubei, to the party Secretariat was defeated. His backdown in the Cuban crisis in October meant a comeback of hard-liners. Sundry initiatives in world affairs, from pressure on Berlin and the wooing of the underdeveloped world to missiles in Cuba, had been costly failures. Eastern Europe was in ferment, the Communist movement was in disarray, and the Sino-Soviet split was widening. The economy, especially agriculture, was in trouble.

By 1964 a large number of high party leaders were unhappy with the policies of Khrushchev. His personality cult was budding, the celebration of his birthday in April meriting eleven pages of *Pravda*; but opposition in the Presidium became overwhelming. A coup was organized quietly in October, and it was sprung while Khrushchev was out of town. He appealed angrily from the Presidium to the Central Committee, which had saved him before; but his supposed friends and dependents there also turned against him.

DICTATORSHIP SANS DICTATOR

Within hours of the announcement that N.S. Khrushchev had resigned for reasons of age and health, his pictures were taken down and his works were being removed from bookstores. Since then, his name has rarely been printed in the Soviet Union and little explanation has been given for his deposition.

Khrushchev's ouster was a Kremlin coup in which the masses were considered to have no legitimate interest and to which they reacted entirely passively. Within the framework of party rules, however, it was constitutional. The Presidium voted to remove Comrade Khrushchev as First Secretary. The matter was referred to the Central Committee, highest policy-making body of the party in the absence of a congress. There were denunciatory speeches and the defendant spoke long and angrily. He was voted down by a large majority. For the first time in

Russian history, a ruler was removed from office by legal and nonviolent means. It was also indicative of political maturity that Khrushchev, although made an unperson, was given a good pension and apartment.

The new men of the top leadership were about ten years younger than Khrushchev. Although of lower class origin, they had fairly advanced technical education. Leonid Brezhnev, the new party leader, Aleksei Kosygin, new Chairman of the Council of Ministers or premier, and Nikolai Podgorny, who in 1965 succeeded Mikoyan as formal president, were graduates respectively of metallurgical, textile, and food processing institutes. They witnessed the revolution and civil war as children only. The new leaders were strictly products of Stalinism; most secured their real start in the purges.

The anonymous committee regime which they headed seemed cautious and sensible. Economic planning became more modest and realistic and there were no more grand schemes. Utopianism dropped from sight. There was an unprecedented quiet on the political scene, with apparent mutual respect of members of the elite. It seemed that the Soviet Union was moving toward an authoritarianism like that of the last tsars, with a government committed to legality and fairly broad freedom except for those who attacked the existing order.

But from the spring of 1965 many measures pointed to a return to orthodoxy and a reduction of freedom. There began a restoration of Stalin's image, especially in regard to his qualities as a war leader, and de-Stalinization was found to hurt ideological education. Peaceful coexistence seemed half-forgotten (unless defined as "a form of ideological struggle"), and the doctrine of "different roads to socialism," with its corollary of peaceful transition, was allowed to lapse. In 1968 and after there was a stiffening of ideological terms with a return to Stalinist positions: unequivocal presentation of the world as scene of titanic struggle of capitalism and socialism, and the thesis of intensifying class struggle as the victory of the workers approached. Brezhnev sustained the necessity of the dictatorship of the proletariat along the whole road from capitalism to socialism. The Lenin cult became exaggerated, especially in the two-year campaign of preparation for the supreme event, his hundredth birthday in April, 1970. Military-patriotic themes were inflated more than ever before in peacetime. The security forces were glorified as champions of socialism against insidious enemies.

From late summer of 1965, there were arrests of "bourgeois nationalists," especially in the Ukraine. Writers came under pressure; two of them, Siniavsky and Daniel, were sentenced to forced labor for publishing abroad stories not acceptable to Soviet censorship. Occasionally thereafter dissenters were imprisoned or consigned to mental hospitals. Repression continued to be far milder than under Stalin, but the collective leadership did not shrink from using force against dissenters. Although there was no return to Stalinist isolation, foreign contacts were checked. Jamming of foreign broadcasts was resumed in August, 1968. Communication between leadership and people was also reduced. The blanket of secrecy over political affairs became denser, as policy disagreements among the top leadership were kept from public view. The dozen or so top leaders rarely appeared in public except on formal or ceremonial occasions, and their utterances seldom betrayed a personal opinion; the best informed observers had few ideas about who stood for what. Some, headed by Kosygin, seemed to have a more practical orientation, apparently favoring consumer goods and detente; others, headed by Brezhnev, indicated a more party-ideological bent. But there seemed to be no fixed alignments.

Brezhnev, as party leader, seems to have been able to promote his friends and so gradually gained a clear ascendancy. At the Twenty-Third Party Congress, in April, 1966, which was far more disciplined than the 1961 Congress, he received the title of General Secretary, which was Stalin's badge of authority. He was the only leader whose dicta were frequently cited as ideological verities. The Twenty-Fourth Party Congress, April, 1971, rang with praise for the General Secretary and cries of "Glory!" to his name. The four additions then made to the Politburo, Kunaev, Kulakov, Grishin, and Shcherbitsky, may have all been Brezhnev protegés. As a personality, Brezhnev has given an impression of outstanding dullness; but it became the norm in almost any public statement to make a bow to him.

More than ever, the party as an entity has been raised up as master of state, economy, and culture, as teacher of the peoples and guardian of ideology, responsible for discipline and unity. Power was drawn back to the center after the timorous previous steps to spread it out in the interests of efficiency. The equalitarian educational changes of Khrushchev were undone. There was less catering to popular sentiment and mass participation. More attention was given to indoctrination than ever before, as the people were called upon to exercise vigilance and even physicists and composers were summoned to contribute to the war of ideas against the West.

Gone from the state, however, was the revolutionary ethos. It had been taken for granted that social transformation, admittedly still incomplete, was the goal of the Soviet leadership; but even the modest proposals of change of the Khrushchev era seem forgotten. The entire structure has grown stiff; the bureaucratic principle of tenure seems prevalent. Of the 1966 Central Committee, four-fifths were continued in 1971. Dismissals from and admissions to the inner circle have been rare indeed. Many ministers have been in office for twenty years or more. No other major government is so stable and so old. Reforms are slow and labored; oligarchic rule seems to mean avoidance of potentially divisive decisions. In conservative spirit, the government greatly increased expenditures of scarce capital for the restoration of historical monuments, returning tsarist palaces to their dazzling splendor for the inspiration of the people.

The Soviet Union has not shared in the trend taken for granted in the Western world in recent decades, the trend toward participation of broader circles in discussion of, if not formulation of policy, greater equality, and more questioning of values. The political and intellectual gulf between the Soviet Union and the Western world has failed to narrow, as it seemed to under Khrushchev and as seemed expectable under the imperatives of modern industrial civilization. Increased international tensions, including the war in Vietnam, undoubtedly played a part, encouraging the ideologists and "conservatives." Erosion of Soviet authority in Eastern Europe caused fears not only of loss of control there but also apprehensions lest this might weaken party authority inside the Soviet Union. The invasion of Czechoslovakia at once required ideological justification and seemed, by its success in restoring party control, to vindicate the use of force.

More fundamentally, the party seems to have resolved to check developments which, if they had continued as in the years 1956-1964, would have eventually resulted in the end of the Soviet system as Stalin built it. The leadership wishes to modernize, as Khrushchev did, but makes an extra effort of control and indoctrination to prevent modernization from loosening the Soviet order.

PART TWO

HOW
THE SOVIET STATE
IS GOVERNED

CHAPTER 6

Ideology and its Uses

All states and all political movements indulge in ideology to some degree, if by ideology one understands a set of ideas sustained for political utility. In this sense, ideology consists of the generalities which political leaders want people to believe, a set of propositions beyond challenge which can be used as a basis for reasoning. It is at once a statement of purposes, cause for self-righteousness, and political rhetoric. This does not imply that ideology is necessarily untrue in any objective sense, but its factual basis is less important than its political usefulness.

If all states take on something of an ideological garb, some have a stronger penchant for it. In capitalist, liberal, and constitutional states there has to be agreement on the constitutional fundamentals and acceptance of certain modes of political action and basic values, but there may be agreement on little else. A loose, pluralistic state can hardly be very ideological. But political absolutism engenders intellectual absolutism. This may be almost mechanical, as rulers of a strong state are in a position to exclude what they deem harmful and to propagate what seems suitable, and it would be naive to expect them to refrain. Aside from the propensity to employ power for their own benefit, all-powerful leaders consider it their duty to inculcate correct views and to exclude harmful ones. Moreover, pure force is insufficient as a means of control; obedience is not complete unless it is voluntary. There is also an imperative demand for an integrative belief system in states lacking in natural unity, like the multinational Soviet Union, and in states suffering social strains from rapid and uneven modernization. Ideology is called upon to help govern the otherwise ungovernable. Hundreds of thousands of persons are full-time purveyors of it in the USSR, and it is a part-time activity of millions. A large part of the attention of party bodies at all levels is given to indoctrination and to the improvement of ideological qualifications, attention fully comparable to that directly applied to the guidance of industry and agriculture.

MARXISM

The bundle of ideas which comprise the Soviet ideology are based on Marxism. Just what Marxism is defies definition. Karl Marx lived long, wrote prolifically, and, being intelligent, changed his ideas through the years. The works of his collaborator, Friedrich Engels, are also sometimes considered part of the Marxist canon. As a doctrine of the nineteenth century, Marxism cannot be applied to the twentieth without substantial modification; and Marxism has been developed in as many directions as there are outstanding Marxists.

The main propositions of Marxism, however, are rather simple and compact. They cover philosophy, history, economics, and politics, all tied together by an emphasis on material tools and relations to production. Marxist philosophy is materialistic; matter is primary and ideas or spirit secondary. This materialism, however, is qualified by somewhat mystical Hegelian principles of dialectic, whereby movement and change are intrinsic in matter. Change proceeds in a jagged forward direction, with a condition, or "thesis" (for example, capitalism) giving rise to an "antithesis" (the growth of the proletariat and the workers' movement) and conflict (revolution) from which there emerges a new "synthesis" (socialism or communism).

The materialistic view of the universe supported a materialistic view of human nature and society. Marx saw men motivated above all by desire for gain; hence, the great fact of social life was their organization around the means of production of wealth. The important divisions, consequently, were of economic classes, determined by how people stood in relation to means of production. It was assumed that the owners of the means of production—factories, land, etc.—were the real bosses, and that they would use their control of the state to squeeze the workers, paying a bare minimum in wages and appropriating the fruit of the toil of the many for themselves. As Marx saw the exploitation of the factory and mine workers of early-industrial England, this was only realistic.

The Marxian interpretation of history followed a similar logic. When means of production were few and readily procured, the primitive form of society must have been communistic, with free and easy sharing of the few goods available; there was hence no coercive power or state. The growth of specialized production and increased importance of wealth led to more complicated and exploitative institutions, the subordination of the many to the few, and slaveholding societies, like the Roman empire. When slavery became unsuitable (for unclear reasons), it was replaced by feudalism, appropriate for agricultural economies. Further development of means of production and trade nourished within the feudal order a mercantile or "bourgeois" class; when the bourgeoisie gained sufficient wealth and strength, it rebelled against the feudal order, notably in the French Revolution. But bourgeois-capitalist society in turn nourished a contrary force within itself, the working class. According to Marx, the workers would become more and more numerous, stronger and stronger. Finally, capitalism would collapse in crises and contradictions of overproduction and lack of markets, of overconcentration and inability to adapt to the needs of an age when production was de facto socialized.

The postulated replacement of capitalism by socialism formed the basis of a political program. The workers, disciplined and class-conscious because of their conditions of labor, could make a selfless socialist order because they had no important property interests. When its historical hour had struck, the proletariat should shake off its bonds and usher in the new era of history—which should happily be the last, the end of history as previously experienced, because there would be no more antagonistic classes.

Marx hardly explained how the socialist society was to be ordered, but the proletarian revolution became the central concern of Marxism, the focus around which all else revolved. Marxism has dual aspects: inevitable development through economic forces is combined with voluntaristic furthering of the revolution. Insistence on the importance of political action separated Marx from his socialist predecessors and made his arid philosophic and historical theories and economic interpretations interesting and relevant. It is fair to agree with Lenin that when Social Democrats ceased to be preoccupied with revolution they ceased to be true Marxists.

Marx was much more concerned with the cause, the liberation and happiness of humanity, than with strict logical consistency. But he struck a responsive chord in attacking the intolerable conditions of factory labor in early industrialization, when humanitarian consciousness was rising against capitalist laissez-faire and calling for governmental intervention to protect the deprived. In an age of burgeoning science, his was the political approach which most strongly claimed to be scientific. In an age of progress and optimism, Marx saw history moving inexorably to an age of perfect order, when work would be a joy, strife would be no more, and all should share freely in an abundance of goods. He theorized the eminently desirable into the inevitable.

Marxism spoke with accents of special truth and certain victory to those on the outs with Western society. For men who saw no prospects of advancement by democratic and gradual process, it offered revolution and title to the future. The completion of the circle from primitive communism to the communism of the future appealed to the nostalgia of victims of industrial society for a simpler and purer life. This feeling had something to do with the receptivity of Russia (and other industrializing countries) to Marxism as an answer to their troubles of social disorganization.

Consequently, the greatest attraction of Marxism was and is not for the lands to which it was logically applicable but for the less developed countries for which capitalism was alien and disliked, and especially for their semiwesternized intellectuals, who found themselves at odds both with the backwardness of their native societies and with the intrusion into them of the capitalist West. They saw a capitalism growing up like the cruder early industrial capitalism which Marx criticized, and Marx gave them a powerful means of attacking it and Western values while adhering to a modern and seemingly scientific creed. Hence the Russian intelligentsia around the turn of the century was far more Marxist in its thinking than that of England or France, or even Germany, where a relatively backward political system gave more scope for Marxism than in countries farther west. And Lenin was prepared to adapt Marxist ideas to Russian conditions.

MARXISM-LENINISM IN USE

As stated earlier, Lenin remade Marxism in several ways. He fitted the discontented peasantry and the national minorities into his revolutionary program. He developed a theory of imperialism to make capitalism responsible for World War I and to justify starting the world socialist revolution in backward Russia. He would not wait for the proletariat to become revolutionary but wanted it to be directed by the party. The proletariat became, then, not the mover of revolution but an instrument, along with others, for the mostly nonproletarian party leadership to use in making revolution and establishing the "dictatorship of the proletariat." Lenin reversed the relation between the economic base and the state form. Now the people, or the party, would make the state and social order by political will.

This ideology for revolution in Russia was little changed when the movement turned from radical attack on the state to the defense and use of state power. Having accepted the task of building a state, Lenin endeavored generally to sustain the original picture of the Russian Revolution serving as the opening skirmish of the world proletarian revolution, in which the Russian workers were acting as part of a universal movement. Stalin renounced obligations to the world movement, but retained it as legitimation and certified that what was being constructed in Russia was indeed socialism and a service to the cause of universal socialism.

Stalin subsequently gave ideological justifications for major policies. Collectivization of agriculture was presented as a substitution of socialized for private property, and the destruction of the prosperous peasants was justified by equating them with capitalist exploiters. By eliminating the independent peasantry and by industrializing, Stalin gave the Soviet Union a class structure more appropriate for a state denominating itself "socialist."

Stalin also settled the Soviet ideological picture by eliminating all independent Marxist thought and decreeing ideology to suit policies. Thus, the priority of heavy industry under planning, and by implication the preference for strength over welfare, became a "law of socialist economy." Strengthening of the repressive powers of the state, which many Bolsheviks had assumed was to wither away not long after the revolution, and hence the purges themselves, were justified by a new theory of the sharpening of the class struggle with the advent of socialism. The equalitarianism sacred to the revolutionary ethos became "petty-bourgeois." Ideology came to cover far more ground than under Lenin; the correct literary approach, the right style of painting, and the proper interpretation of pre-Soviet history, etc. were decreed by more or less explicit fiat. The genetics of Lysenko, the most rational part of which was the supposed inheritance of acquired characteristics, was true by Stalinist sanction.

Khrushchev wanted to make ideology more useful by making it more modern and realistic. But he thereby denatured it politically. In his interpretation, "practical" Marxism-Leninism became little more than action to increase production, coupled with a vision of Soviet greatness in the world. He would have made economic growth the basic inspiration, filling the role of Lenin's revolution and Stalin's social transformation. The road to communism laid out by the 1961 Program was defined largely in terms of increased production, with little structural change beyond some transfer of additional responsibility from state organs to "public" party-dominated organizations.

The collective leadership confronted the problem of ideology in a somewhat different spirit. The revolutionary generation had largely departed; the storming of the Winter Palace and the travails of civil war were only history to an increasingly sophisticated younger generation. "Class struggle" and "proletariat" had become almost meaningless abstractions to many or most of the people. Hence the concept of "proletariat" was broadened to include "not only factory workers, engaged in physical labor, but those who contribute intellectual labor or carry on various auxiliary functions."[1] "Class struggle" was wholly projected onto the foreign scene. Domestically there remained little drive to change, unless perhaps for the perfection and strengthening of party leadership. To replace fading revolutionary emotions, the leadership has stressed symbolism, the father-figure of Lenin, military discipline, past heroics, history, and patriotism. It has also intensified ideological work and efforts toward indoctrination, reverting toward Leninist and Stalinist fundamentalism. There is to be no thought of compromise; East-West bridge building was branded "imperialist subversion" and the theory of convergence of capitalism and communism was exposed as a weapon of anti-Sovietism.

USES OF IDEOLOGY: LEGITIMATION

By Marxism, there are no absolute moral or legal standards, only expressions of class interest. The ruling class defines truth and justice, and any other pretense is only a fraud. The proletariat, however, has a superior right to rule because it is the class destined by history to succeed to the leadership of society and because it supposedly represents the large majority against the handful of exploiters. Moreover, it is morally superior by virtue of its freedom from the corruption of capital.

In the Soviet system the party exercises the rights of the workers in their name. The core of Marxism-Leninism thus became the party's right and duty to rule. Any opposition could be stigmatized as weakening the sacred cause of the workers. The party should be arbiter of right and wrong and maker of values. The claim to know the will of the workers themselves is based on the party's possession of the truths of "scientific socialism." Political truth, like facts of chemistry, is held to be knowable and unequivocal for the experts who are the rulers. Marxism-Leninism is treated as a rigorous science, embracing laws of historical development, socialist revolution, dictatorship of the proletariat, and the laws of construction of socialist society.

Acceptance of the party's leadership and its perceptions is mandatory because the world scene is one of perpetual struggle between the forces of light and dark. In theory, there is an everlasting semimilitary emergency, in which the achievements of socialism increase the hostility of its enemies and make relaxation the more dangerous. Nothing could be more important than this war wherein the glorious and happy future seeks to overcome the evil past, to overthrow the last exploiting class, and bring the prophesied paradise. It justifies whatever the party may demand.

It is doubtful how seriously the elite takes the Marxist vision of material abundance sufficient to satiate human desires, total harmony reigning, and all toiling joyously for the good of society. But the fundamentals of the Soviet way are inherent in utopianism: an elite to lead the way, a monopoly of truth to guide it, and an evil (capitalism) to be slain in saving mankind. Devotion is to a supreme cause, the perfection of Man through the perfection of the political order. It becomes less important what happens to individuals in the process.

The greatest step toward utopia is the socialization, or ownership, of the economy by the people or the state. This is the essential characteristic of the socialist society, and it is at the same time the prime underpinning of the power of the party. Ownership of means of production, as Marxists emphasize, gives leverage over people. To deprive any possible opposition of an economic base the party socializes as much as possible and leaves as little as possible outside of its control. Anyone seeking to subsist irregularly, outside the framework of control, is subject to the charge of parasitism, or failure to contribute to the community in a recognized fashion. Hence the ideological antipathy for private money-making and individual commerce, despite its obvious potential contribution to the standard of living. Hence also the urge for centralization, bigger enterprises being easier to control. If only money could be eliminated, all goods would be distributed by some sort of political authorization or order; and economic differences would disappear, leaving only differences of status.

To speak of the workers toiling for themselves in socialist enterprise implies that they have deep obligations to "their" enterprises. If they labor for low wages, this cannot be exploitation but service to the community. The terminology of "people's" factories is suggestive; Russians consider it less demeaning to work for the incorporated community than for a private owner whose interest is frankly gain. The economic progress which has marked the Soviet era serves further to legitimate the party which has presided over it.

The broadly collectivist spirit of Marxism and indeed of Russian tradition also serves the party interest. "The basis of our life, as is well known, is collectivism."[2] To be individualistic is to be selfish and bourgeois. "Everything is done so that the individual, from the first to the last day of his life, should feel the care of the collective around him, not only in regard to his material but also his spiritual needs."[3] "Individualism and egoism, rapacious thirst for gain. . . these are the traits which the bourgeois world inculcates with its private property . . . Our society raises a really new man, the collectivist, fighter, builder, patriot and internationalist."[4] Even scientists should esteem collective above individual thinking. This appeal to instincts of solidarity and release from loneliness merges into a call for limitless unity: collective, party, the Soviet people, the world communist movement, and ultimately all virtuous people of all races, all toilers. Collectivism should foster the conviction that service to the state is honor and glory. Soviet citizens, having given their all at their jobs, are expected to volunteer frequently and in large numbers for all manner of community endeavors, from cleaning up around buildings to acting as part time guardians of public order; the materialistic religion of Marxism-Leninism calls for devotion beyond material interests.

Socialism further shields the party and state from suspicion of selfishness. By definition, only private ownership can be exploitative; tyranny can only be of a possessing class. The Soviet state is consequently pure; it can represent only virtue because it stands for the virtuous working class and there is no need to check its power. Politics, moreover, is excluded in principle, because political conflict can be only a reflection of class conflict. Any political action outside the party must represent, in some subterfuge, a class enemy attack; nor can there be admitted any political contest within the party.

USES OF IDEOLOGY: ISOLATION

Ideology serves as the spiritual or psychological foundation of the wall between Soviet and foreign societies, especially shutting out insidious influences of the West. It achieves this in part by exalting the Socialist Fatherland and its works; everything in Soviet life should be practically by definition different and better. Russia is the center of history; as the formal chief of state, Podgorny, has it, "We live in an epoch when all the most important historical changes in the world are connected with the Great October socialist revolution . . ."[5]

On the other hand, the "capitalist" world, or at least its leading and more powerful sectors, are viewed as black. The hallmarks of "bourgeois" society are egoism, individualism, anarchism, lewdness, hedonism, unemployment, injustice, violence, and imperialism; capitalism is synonymous with venality and inhumanity. Even as individuals, "socialists" have a near-monopoly of virtue; no one of the "bourgeoisie" could be generous or heroic, although friends of the Soviet Union are "progressive." "Proletarian" and "bourgeois" democracy, nationalism, law, etc., are not similar but opposites, and the latter are beyond redemption. Corporations are always referred to as "monopolies." The apparatus of representative government in the West is seen as mere cover for the dictatorship of capital. No credit is given for reforms. At best, concessions are exacted by the indignation of the people; and if the state seems to become more socialistic by increasing public ownership and control of the economy, this is a deception. Marxist socialists can congratulate themselves on being humanitarian and unselfish, while their antagonists are grasping and malicious, misled by their backward political and social structure. In the view of ordinary Soviet citizens, free education, pensions, and democracy, meaning the ability of workers to improve themselves, are out of the question under capitalism, which means racial discrimination, unemployment, disorder, and war.

"Bourgeois" serves as a convenient label for anything disapproved, such as a call for freer debate within the party. Critical writers can be held up as agents of "imperialism", and "bourgeois mentality" is a generic term for incorrect thinking. The theme of world struggle has been useful in a hundred ways, from Stalin's terrorism to the rejection of Solzhenitsyn. The latter responded in a letter to the Writers' Union: " 'The enemy is listening.' That's your answer. These eternal enemies are the basis of your existence. What would you do without your enemies? You would not be able to live without your enemies. Hate, hate no less evil than racism, has become your sterile atmosphere. But in this way the feeling of a whole and single mankind is being lost and its perdition is being accelerated."[6]

So far as the masses learn to think in basically class terms, they are protected from notions of nationalism, "bourgeois" freedom, civil rights, and the like. It is even more essential to protect the intellectuals from the Western ideas to which they are inevitably exposed. After long years of education in Marxist-Leninist categories it becomes difficult for them to understand Western political arguments and values. To the extent that this can be achieved, the party has solved a fundamental problem of Russian government, borrowing what is useful while keeping out subversive individualistic or libertarian influences.

Marxism-Leninism seems effective as a psychological weapon. It forms a unified world view and a fairly coherent body of doctrine, parts of which are difficult to challenge without rejecting the whole structure. Though students may be bored by the dialectical materialism they are required to study, it can hardly fail to become the framework of their thinking about social and political questions. It is not easy for Soviet citizens to understand "bourgeois" concepts of political rights, and hardly any are theoretical advocates of economic liberalism.

USES OF IDEOLOGY: UNITY

One of the most vital ways in which Marxism-Leninism serves the Soviet system is the furnishing of an elastic concept, the working class, to bridge the cleavages of Soviet society. This is implied, in part, by the polarization of the world and the contraposition of Soviet socialism to imperialism and the class enemy without. More specifically, however, Marxism-Leninism decrees that differences such as those of religion or nationality are false and bourgeois-manufactured, whereas all Soviet citizens are really united in belonging to the broadly-defined working people, builders of communism.

Class bonds should overcome all divisions, particularly those of religion and nationality. The gravest are those of nationality. Russians proper are only about half the total population—those of authentic Russian background probably are a good deal less. Of the remainder, some are fairly close to the "Great Russians," like the Belorussians and Ukrainians, once called "Little Russians"; but many others are quite alien in culture, language, and religion. In particular, the Turkic peoples of Central Asia form a fairly homogeneous and indigestible group of some thirty million. The Soviet Union is the last great multinational domain in a world of growing national awareness of minority and dominated peoples. Marxism-Leninism is a faith which can be taught as a basis of morality and philosophy to Turks, Balts, Mongols, and others on the same basis, as a neutral, supposedly scientific creed, unencumbered by particular association with Russians and russification. It also lays a blanket of class community over differences of nationality. The authentic separation, according to Marxism, is between classes, between exploiters and exploited, not between nations; in the classic aphorism, the workers have no country. Hence, in the Soviet view, nationalism is bourgeois poison; all the peoples must be firmly united because the proletariat must be united. "The working class . . . is the cement that holds together our monolithic multinational state."[7] Any suggestion of separatism is treason to the class cause. There can be no licit opposition to the Soviet Union, which represents the brotherhood of peoples building socialism against the opposition of the class enemy. The ideal of socialism also serves to override nationalism. Ownership is vested in the central regime, and Moscow is the center of planning and much administration. To permit private enterprise would be to invite the creation of local power centers supporting divisive tendencies.

Loyalty to the working class should override any nationalistic tendencies in Eastern Europe as within the Soviet Union. Proletarian internationalism gave the Soviet Union and allied states the right, indeed the duty, to intervene in Czechoslovakia in 1968. According to a

Pravda commentator, "Nationalism under contemporary conditions is expressed above all in overlooking the basic contradiction of our era, the contradiction between socialism and capitalism, in the rejection of class positions . . ."[8] According to the Czech premier installed by the Russians, "Such concepts as freedom, democracy, have their class content, class forms. Where this is lost, and the class approach to problems is dulled, there rises a nationalistic wave."[9]

In practice, the workers have usually seemed at least as aware of belonging to a nation as to a class. The nation is a much better defined group than the class; it is easier to draw lines between Frenchmen and Germans than to divide either into "workers" and "bourgeois." It is also likely that an Uzbek worker may feel more in common with Uzbek intellectuals than with Russian immigrants into his country, whether blue or white collar workers. Ideology has by no means solved the Soviet nationality problem, and there is considerable evidence of continuing, perhaps increasing self-awareness of peoples and discontent with centralization and alien domination. But the party's answer has been at least partially successful, and it has no other.

Unity is the central meaning of Soviet ideology with loyalty, nominally to the cause but actually to the party, overriding all else. This is the bedrock, the deepest apparent commitment of the party leadership, the first principle of party organization, perhaps the supreme value of the political system. Of all threats to Soviet unity, the gravest is that of national separation. It may be, consequently, that this is the largest single factor dictating the remarkable persistence of a revolutionary proletarian class doctrine as the official creed of a state which has long ceased to be either revolutionary or proletarian in spirit. If there were no Russian minorities problem, the world would have heard much less of Karl Marx during the past half century.

LENINISM AND DUTY

Marxism-Leninism is embarrassing for the conservative, hierarchic Soviet state. The basic ideas of Marxism are proletarianism and revolution;

yet in Russia today a social chasm lies between the elite and the manual worker. Marxism outside the Communist sphere continues to be an inspiration for the overthrow of the established order, but the Soviet has become an established order. Marxism lacks emotional relevance for Soviet citizens, and offers nothing for the crises of life. As its utopia recedes it holds little for the idealism of youth. The Soviet leadership consequently has turned to supplement increasingly anemic Marxist doctrines with symbolism, collectivist emotions, and social discipline, themes appropriate for the solidification of society. Marxism often seems overshadowed by the glorious history of the party and of the Socialist Fatherland and the Russian homeland before it, by the call for community and patriotic devotion, and by Leninolatry.

V.I. Lenin is chief of the Soviet pantheon. Everyone is urged to read his works; Lenin is the greatest of world thinkers, an ultimate authority on anything. The Leninist scriptures are a canon (somewhat like "Mao Tse-tung thought") to which little has been added despite the recognized need for developing Marxism-Leninism for the changed Soviet reality of today. A quote from Lenin may be used to support any policy, including some of which he disapproved such as tight controls on literature.

Lenin is even more of an inspiring personality than a doctrinal authority. His biography and the countless tales of his deeds or of meeting him are hagiography. "Lenin—every photograph, preserving his inimitable features for the ages, is priceless—"[10] and much used. Especially inspiring is how Lenin came down sometimes like a god from Olympus to help the humble in their toil. He cannot be really dead; the motto is, "Lenin lives." As school children chanted for the Twenty-Fourth Party Congress,

> "Lenin lives, Lenin lives
> In thoughts and deeds and hearts of the people!
> He teaches to live and conquer
> Never to retreat
> To go to the glowing horizons
> And we can proudly say
> Lenin today
> Is in this hall!"[11]

Like Stalin, Lenin has been made into the symbol of unity, justice, and the authority of the party. "When we say 'Lenin,' we understand 'the party,' when we say 'the party' we understand 'Lenin'."[12] He is frequently designated as "the leader" ("vozhd"), a term of authoritarian overtones formerly applied to Stalin. His usually stern countenance, sometimes in gigantic busts or portraits, looks down on almost every worker and every public event. To save a statue of Lenin from desecration is a feat worth risking one's life.[13] The two-year preparations for Lenin's hundredth birthday in April, 1970, "an immense event in the history of humanity," as the Russians put it, were by far the biggest anniversary commemorations of history.* Almost everyone in the Soviet Union was supposed to contribute in some way, overfulfilling plans in his honor or studying his life and works. For months, Lenin filled books and periodicals, and more than a dozen full-length movies illumined his life for Soviet viewers.

The apotheosis of Lenin merges into the glorification of his Bolshevik party both before the revolution and after, when it becomes practically the history of the Soviet Union. Through its struggles, the party has incarnated the virtues of the proletariat. The heroic chapters of its struggle are rehearsed and reviewed: the revolution, victory in civil war, the First Five-Year Plan, collectivization, victory in the Fatherland War, and postwar reconstruction and the building of socialism. Basically united despite the need from time to time to expel bad elements, the party remains infallible. Resting its legitimacy more upon tradition and less upon mission of change, the regime stresses its roots in a sacred past.

The heroism of military struggles gives an aura of glory to Soviet history, not only in the making of the revolution and the civil war but even more in the essentially nationalistic Great Patriotic War of 1941-1945, wherein the Russian, Soviet, and Communist emotions are fused. With the flood of stories and memoirs has swelled the glorification of military ways and virtues, discipline and self-sacrifice, in a spirit much closer to Prussianism than Marxism. Newspapers are commonly graced with one or more pieces about the brave and handsome defenders of

---

*The actual day, April 27, was celebrated by staying at work.

the fatherland. Soviet discourse is thick with military metaphors; brigadiers and shock workers storm fortresses, etc. There is a certain grimness in the Soviet outlook, with emphasis on the conquest of socialism drowning out the idea of its enjoyment. The Soviet citizen should not primarily look forward to the Marxist heaven but should think mostly of giving his all and his life if necessary for its attainment. Fear for onesself and family, a Soviet medical scientist finds, is very bad for the heart, but fear of death or suffering for a just cause strengthens the organism.[14]

The Soviet official philosophy thus suffers an acute two-sidedness, as it stands for revolution and change in the world yet for stability and coherence at home. The Russians give the fullest moral support to youthful protesters in the capitalist world yet combat hippyism at home; antiwar demonstrators in the United States are thus portrayed as the best Boy Scout types. There is an inherent contradiction between the oft cited virtues of Soviet patriotism and "proletarian internationalism." But both rationalize and strengthen the Soviet system of party rule.

FOOTNOTES

1. *Pravda*, December 24, 1968.
2. *ibid*, February 27, 1971.
3. *Selskaia zhizn*, October 22, 1969.
4. *Pravda* editorial, March 15, 1970.
5. *ibid*, November 7, 1969;
6. *New York Times*, November 15, 1969.
7. *Krasnaia zvezda*, May 21, 1971.
8. *Pravda*, January 15, 1969.
9. *ibid*, August 22, 1969.
10. *ibid*, February 8, 1970.
11. *ibid*, April 2, 1971.

12. *ibid,* April 26, 1970.
13. *ibid,* October 29, 1969.
14. *Sovetskaia Rossiia,* October 25, 1970.

CHAPTER 7

The Party, Holder of Power

ORGANIZATION

Ideology, which sets forth basic purposes and the relations of the party to Soviet society, is what the party says it is and is inseparable from the party organization which should make it effective. If ideology is the word, the party is the organizational incarnation thereof, the one claiming monopoly of truth, the other, monopoly of organization.

Just as the heart of Soviet ideology is loyalty to the will of the party as the incorporation of right and justice, the central principle of the Communist party of the Soviet Union (and of the many Leninist parties patterned after it) is the maximum mobilization of wills in the name of ideology. This means a structure whereby smaller numbers dominate larger groups in a series of circles downward and outward. Thus at the top the twenty-five men of the Politburo together with the Secretariat oversee the Central Committee of nearly four hundred and the central apparatus, and at each lower level the secretariat or the "buro" manages the party committee. The party organization in Moscow thus guides the republic and provincial organizations, and these in turn guide organizations of smaller territorial units, and so down to the primary party organizations in factories and farms. At each level, relatively few party men watch over and to some extent direct much larger numbers of leaders in governmental, cultural, and other nonparty organizations. A minority leads and guides the majority again at the bottom, as party fractions within organizations assure conformity to party policy; overall, the minority of party members guide the entirety of Soviet society.

As a ruling group, however, the party is large. It has tended to grow throughout Soviet history except for the purges after 1921 and 1933, expansion being most rapid when there was felt most need for support, as in the months prior to the revolution, in the civil war, and in the Second World War. Since solidification of the Soviet regime after 1939, growth has been steady. It accelerated under Khrushchev but since 1966 has slowed somewhat. At the beginning of 1971 there were 14,400,000 members, about one-tenth of the adult population.

Generally speaking, the better one's status in Soviet society, the easier it is to become a party member. The "best people," the top layers in organizations and professions, are expected to be in the party. Likewise workers of special skills and in prestigious branches of production are more likely to be invited to join than low-grade workers. But enough persons of low occupational status are taken in to preserve appearances of proletarianism.

The would-be party member applies where he works. He must be recommended by three party members in good standing with at least five years' service. Young persons up to the age of twenty-three (eighteen being the minimum) may join only through the Komsomol, which in recent years has furnished about half of party entrants. A person becomes a full member only after a probationary period of one year as "candidate." For full membership endorsement of the next higher party committee is required.

To join the party is like marriage or taking the vows of a religious order, with no provision for resignation. It is a commitment to an active political life and an open road to advancement according to ambition, devotion, and capacities. "Above all, every entrant into the CPSU should deeply understand that from this moment he is representative of a ruling party, the guiding force in the state, which lays enormous responsibility on him. This means that he must live by Leninist principles; that means, the interests of the party first, everything else is secondary."[1] He subscribes to a "Moral Code of a Communist" that is practically religious in its commandments of loyalty, love of the cause, and moral perfection. The member must be a model citizen and worker, spread the party ideals, receive humbly any criticism, follow injunctions, accept any assignments and volunteer for more. His happiness should be toil and struggle.

The member is directly responsible to his basic party organization in a factory, school, or collective farm. There are some 350,000 primary party organizations, with membership from three to a thousand or more. Those with over fifty members are likely to be subdivided by shop, section, or department, with as many as three lower layers of divisions or groups. Primary organizations always have a secretary as responsible head, but the number and kind of committees and staff varies greatly with size. In a typical factory organization of 150 members there will be one elected secretary with two understudies, one for organization, the other for agitation and propaganda, supported by a buro of a dozen, backed up by an "aktiv," a more eager and responsible minority. Buro members specialize in various areas of party activity, such as production, volunteer work, youth organization, propaganda, etc.

The party narrows upward by stages corresponding to administrative divisions, from the primary organization to borough, city, or county, then to the provincial level and to the republic (except for the Russian republic, which has no party organization of its own) and to the All-Union level. The formal structure (see chart pp. 104-5) is fairly simple in principle. Party members elect or rubber-stamp the choice of delegates to a city or county ("raion") conference, every two or three years according to the rules. The conference forms a committee, which has its inner circle or buro and its secretariat. The conferences also elect delegates to a provincial conference, which likewise has a committee with buro and secretariat. Delegates from conferences proceed to form a congress in the non-Russian republics. Republic congresses and provincial conferences in the Russian republic send delegates to

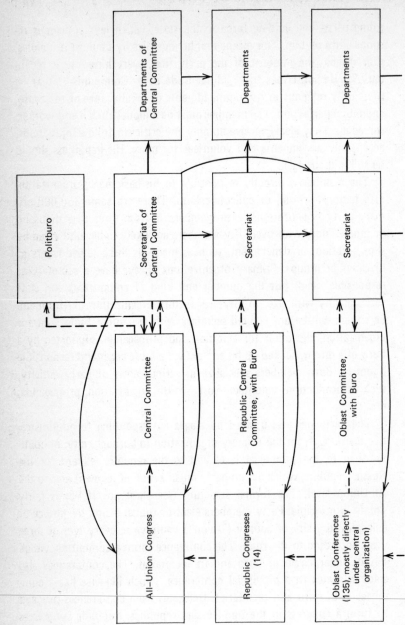

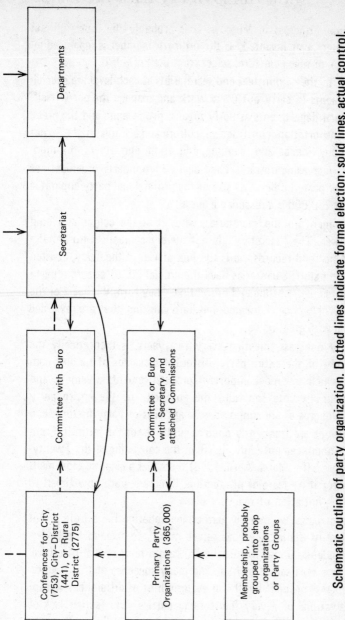

Schematic outline of party organization. Dotted lines indicate formal election; solid lines, actual control.

the All-Union Congress in Moscow. It is probably the most indirect electoral system ever invented, as the ordinary member is separated by as many as six or seven electoral stages from the Politburo.

Attached to the committees and secretariats at each level are specialized departments to carry out party work and manage the party itself. There are such departments as party organs, propaganda and the press, industry, transportation, construction, culture and schools, trade, Soviet administration, finance and planning, education, and others, the number and size increasing upward. They deal with nonparty organizations or with lower party bodies. The size of the professional party apparatus is secret, but 250,000 is a reasonable guess.

The key men are the secretaries, who sit at the center and hold reins of power. The "secretary" is not merely someone who handles correspondence and records; he is the line officer of the party, assisted by troops and staff. Secretaries have the crucial job of selecting party and other personnel, posting and promoting. They form the heart of the new nobility of service. Educated and hard working, they are rewarded for loyal toil with great power.

The party congress, meeting every five years, is theoretically the supreme body of the entire party, historical successor of Lenin's congresses, at which the most important pronouncements are made and whose unanimous vote sanctions the authority of the entire party apparatus. Congresses are supposed to mark eras of party history, and their resolutions are frequently cited as guidance for the faithful. From the time of announcement (July, 1970) of the convening of the Twenty-Fourth Congress (for March-April, 1971) there was a gigantic movement to prepare for it by feats of production. Congresses are now timed to solemnize the initiation of five-year plans.

Early congresses were lively gatherings debating basic policy, but since the rise of Stalin they have served mostly to acclaim the leadership; the tendency under Khrushchev toward a faint revival of critical discussion was reversed after him. The many speeches of the Twenty-Fourth Congress brought hardly an esoteric hint of differences, except in the reservations of a very few foreign parties. The factual lack of power of the congresses is underlined both by the publicity which surrounds them and by their large size, which has grown from the few score of prerevolutionary days to about five thousand.

More important is the Central Committee, which the congress unanimously elects on the suggestion of the leadership. It is legally the supreme authority of the party when a congress is not in session, which is almost all the time. Its membership is often pointed to as the quintessence of the Soviet elite. Currently, it has 396 members, 241 full members and 155 candidates, having gradually swelled from the twenty-three members of 1918. The membership is about four-fifths high party and government officials, the remainder being drawn from all important areas of Soviet life, the military (about a twelfth), police officials, enterprise directors, collective farm chairmen, one or two scientists and writers, and the like. A handful of outstanding workers and farmers are also regularly honored with a place on the Central Committee. Women are only 3% of the membership. The evident principle of selection is to draw together important persons who are concerned with the implementation of party policy in all fields. The Central Committee should meet by statute at least twice yearly, sitting from one to several days.

Attached to the Central Committee is a set of powerful departments. Most influential is that for party organs, which keeps dossiers on all higher positions. That for propaganda trains propagandists and supervises the control of media. About a dozen departments deal with branches of the economy, overseeing respective ministries. Other departments handle science, education, the military, satellite countries, foreign parties, foreign affairs, and party housekeeping. Departments are unpublicized; secrecy is testimony to their importance, in accord with the Soviet rule that publicity is for effect and secrecy for decision-making.

The departments are under the Secretariat, which since 1966 has had ten members. The party rules say of the Secretariat that it is to "direct current work, chiefly the selection of personnel and the verification of the fulfillment of party decisions." Four secretaries are currently full members of the Politburo, two are candidate members. The General Secretary is head of the party but his powers remain veiled. He has his own secretariat to oversee the various departments.

The policy bureau, or Politburo of the Central Committee, set up to guide the revolution, was formalized in 1919; it immediately became the center of decision-making at the expense of the then still manageably small Central Committee. At the Twenty-Fourth Congress the number of full members was increased from eleven to fifteen, supplemented by six candidate members. The Politburo includes leaders of the most important organs of the Communist Party and Soviet state, except the armed forces, and members of important minority nationalities. This body thus serves some representative function and is a sort of collective head of state, acting as honorary presidium of many gatherings.

MANAGEMENT OF THE PARTY

Every effort is made to select men totally devoted to the system of party rule. In accordance with Lenin's original idea, the party is composed of unconditionals, with whom there should be no real problem of control. Yet a great effort is still made through party rules and organization to assure absolute conformity.

"Democratic Centralism" is the basic doctrine of party management. Democratic in appearance and centralist in effect, it permits criticism but places stringent limits on it. Criticism and discussion of policy are permissible only so far as the party has not taken a position on a question. This does not mean that critical and incisive discussion is not desired, but the bounds are very narrow. There is no criticism of those near the top (criticism of high party figures even by their equals is almost invariably indirect and perceptible only to the initiated), no discussion of fundamentals of the Soviet system, no questioning of policies accepted by the party. It is not even permissible to put a question on the agenda without agreement of the authorities. After the decision has been taken, all members are supposed to accept it as their own.

The formation of factions to present different views has been prohibited for fifty years. Any attempt to form an unauthorized grouping is seen as a threat to party unity, leading potentially to independent centers and splits. The rule is strict. Party members are not to address a joint petition to higher-ups; they are limited to speaking individually in official meetings on matters open for discussion and should not talk over any concerted position. In any case, ordinary party members have little basis for criticism because they have no information about how important decisions are reached, what considerations were involved, or who is responsible for them. Different layers of the party are given access to material of differing degrees of confidentiality, just as information is divulged to party members but kept from the general public.

The strongest provision of Democratic Centralism is the requirement of obedience of all lower party bodies to higher ones. The hierarchic authority is much like that of an army. Stalin aptly compared the top ranks of the party to generals, the next layer to officers, and the apparatchiks to noncoms; and the situation in this regard has not changed. Local party bodies are in any case very weak. They have only such funds as the center allows them. "Instructors" attached to party committees advise party bodies below them and sit in on their meetings. Party departments at each level are subject to the corresponding department of the next higher party committee. Each party secretary must be confirmed in office by the next higher party committee.

The democratic aspects of Democratic Centralism are featherweight, intended to foster consensus by serving appearances. One of them is accountability of higher to lower, which means the holding of meetings or conferences at which leaders appear, review achievements, more or less acknowledge shortfalls, and make policy statements. Except occasionally at the lowest level, there seems to be no sharp questioning of superiors by hierarchic inferiors.

The other democratic element of Democratic Centralism is the election of higher bodies by lower ones from the bottom through various stages to the top. Party members have the right, of which they are commonly unaware,[2] to propose and discuss candidates. But there can be no electioneering or even, theoretically, talk of a candidacy in the corridor. A member can speak up only in the regular electoral meeting, conducted under the eagle eye of a superior instructor or secretary, who sits on the presidium to "raise the ideological level," interpret the rules, and propose candidates. Apparently the number of candidates is regularly equal to the number of positions to be filled. The local body may rebel against the suggested nominee to force the naming of another, but this seems to be rare. Any candidate whom the higher-ups dislike can be ordered to withdraw. Or the elections can be annulled. The party electors, in other words, are supposed to act from conviction but to make the approved choice. It would be fair to say that from top down secretaries name their inferiors. Nonetheless, it is a firm obligation of members to participate in elections. The discussion of merits and shortcomings is intended to be educational for both candidates and electors.

There are also ample means for control of the individual Communist. He must obey any decision of his own party organization or of a superior party organization. He is expected to exude virtue and in theory (although practice seems often to be the reverse), he should expect to be punished more severely than ordinary citizens for any infraction. Anything which can be interpreted as "antiparty action" may be cause of disciplinary sanctions. His private life is not private; the party may inquire into his affairs and require penitence for errors. On the other hand, the party may give comradely assistance if he is in trouble of any kind. If one should stray, the penalty may be expulsion, which is almost sure to end a man's career prospects, as the status of an ex-member is much worse than that of a nonmember. There are also reprimands of various degrees of severity which may go into the party book and become a permanent handicap to advancement. Any misstep, although it leads to no formal sanction, may cause an entry in the secret dossier which is kept on each member, like a military personnel record.

Psychological formation also contributes to conformity. It is the duty of Communists not only to teach others but forever to raise their "ideological level." There are countless party schools of various levels, seminars, lectures, and indoctrination sessions. Secretaries attend special courses. Those tapped for promotion are likely to be sent for years to higher party schools to immerse themselves more deeply in Marxism-

Leninism. There must be no complacency, but the member should ever strive for ideological improvement, pondering by day and dreaming by night how better to fulfill the wishes of the party.

By such means, the central core tightly controls the party. At each level, power is concentrated in those next to the chain of command, the buro and especially the secretaries, who manage the *nomenklatura*, a list of positions the filling of which is their responsibility. At all levels, conferences of congresses ratify what has been decided in advance by the apparatus. Debate is guided by the secretaries and speakers are picked in advance; if there is criticism, it is a sign that the victims have already been disgraced.

At the top, the Central Committee is formally supreme, but meets too briefly and infrequently to have much to say about the running of affairs. It serves purposes of legitimation; party decisions are decreed in its name, the secretaries and various committees are attached to it, and it is the officially sovereign head of the party except when a congress meets. It also has functions of coordination and information, as it brings together several hundred of the highest placed officials from various branches of government, party, and important organizations with whom the top leaders find it advantageous, if not indispensable, to consult in regard to execution of policy. Khrushchev permitted some fairly lively debates to take place in the Central Committee; if there have been any since, they have not been publicized.

Power comes to a focus in the Politburo, which appears to be the principal decision-making body. The full members are perhaps the most important individuals in the Soviet Union; candidate membership seems to mean much less. Besides the Politburo there is the Secretariat which also meets weekly, according to Brezhnev. But members of the Politburo generally hold high positions outside the central party apparatus; that is, they are charged with overseeing execution of party policy. The secretaries, on the other hand, rarely have nonparty positions. It is probable that the Politburo is judge of policy but the Secretariat is master of personnel and general party overseer, as suggested by the party rules and can even decide who enters the Politburo. The conspiracy to oust Khrushchev was incubated within the Secretariat, executed by the Politburo, and ratified by the Central Committee; this probably indicates the usual roles of the three bodies.

THE YOUTH AUXILIARY

The organization of youth is important for the mobilization of young people, for ideological training of the oncoming generation, and for the preparation and selection of new recruits for the party. Consequently the Komsomol (officially, "All-Union Leninist League of Communist Youth") is a vital adjunct of the party. Comprising about half of the fourteen to twenty-eight age bracket, or over twenty-seven million youths, the Komsomol organization closely parallels that of the party, from local groups at work places or schools with committees and secretaries, the regional conferences, committees, bureaus, and so forth, up to the big national congress, central committee, buro and secretariat. The intermediate and upper layers are professionals, probably party members, and candidates for careers in the party apparatus. Elections through the Komsomol organization are handled in much the same way as in the party. Females comprise over two-fifths of the membership; but, as in the party, very few have higher positions.

The party rules state that "The Komsomol works under the guidance of the Communist Party of the Soviet Union. The work of the local Komsomol organizations is directed and controlled by the corresponding republican, oblast, district, city and county party organizations." This control is nearly absolute. At the bottom level, party organizations recommend Komsomol leaders. Individual party members are to give the young people the continual benefit of their political maturity; party men attend Komsomol meetings and the two organizations often meet jointly.

In the past, the Komsomol has served as a valuable reserve of volunteer and often enthusiastic labor. In the First Five-Year Plan, many thousands of dedicated youths tackled projects under the most difficult conditions. Recently, the Komsomol was reported to be patronizing a hundred major industrial or construction projects, to which it contributed 300,000 volunteers. Everywhere, Komsomol members are supposed to be examples of eager volunteer work and of steady devotion to their jobs in field or factory.

A more important task of the Komsomol seems to be educational-political, and it carries on many lectures, seminars, and inspirational entertainments, not only for its own members but for nonaffiliated youth and others. It works with military authorities in military training, paramilitary activities, and indoctrination. Komsomol groups in industry and agriculture cooperate with party and trade-union organizations to raise production. The Komsomols provide recruits for the volunteer police helpers; the youthful activists regard themselves as guardians of Soviet orthodoxy and morality. If girls dress immodestly (limits of modesty being rather narrow) or if boys drink too much, the Komsomol is likely to take them in hand, whether they are members or not.

Membership in the Komsomol and its recommendation are practically requisite for admission to a higher institution. The student is subject to Komsomol jurisdiction, not only in regard to political conformity but also in personal behavior.

The Komsomol also provides guidance for the school children, "Young Pioneers," even as the party leads the youth. Members are leaders of Pioneer brigades, which normally include nearly all children in school classes of ages ten to fifteen. The chief effort is directed toward molding the psychology of the future Soviet citizen. Kept busy with wholesome social activities, from games to volunteer jobs to camps, military games, and training, the Pioneers should learn to regard themselves primarily as members of a collective and ultimately of the world Communist movement.

WORK OF THE PARTY

The Soviet state does not consist of legislative, executive, and judicial branches but of the party and its instruments. The government formally based on the soviets is merely one of the means, along with the economic administration, the trade-unions, and other organizations, whereby the party carries out its mission of rule. At times, as under Stalin, the government has seemed to acquire some standing vis-a-vis the party, and during the brief tenure of Malenkov the governmental apparatus seemed to have some importance in its own right. But Khrushchev restored the absolute primacy of the party. Since Khrushchev and especially after 1967 there has been a further elevation of the party, seen more than ever as omnicompetent guide of government, economy, and culture. The party sets broad policies, governmental and economic, and supervises their administration; it leads practically all permitted organizations (the chief exception being some religious groups); it selects responsible personnel in all fields; it propagates ideology and makes, or tries to make morality; so far as possible, it stands at the head of the world Communist movement. It concerns itself with everything from troubles of the Near East to literature, milk production, and bus service.

The party does not merely direct the government and other organizations at the top; it supervises in the republic, province, county, city, village, enterprise and farm. Party organization parallels that of the formal state, making it easy to exert pressure at all levels. In all branches, men should heed the voice of the party more than that of their administrative superiors. The first secretary is the boss of his district and is sometimes referred to as such in Soviet writing. The provincial party organization concerns itself with everything in its area except the armed forces, for which there is a separate and especially elaborate system of control. The leadership thus has an apparatus, unburdened by direct administrative duties, to enforce its will at every stage. This may be the greatest reason why the Soviet Union has managed thus far to keep within bounds the corruption and slackness which cursed the tsarist regime.

The party prefers to persuade rather than to coerce, takes advantage of the monopoly of organization and political leadership, and preserves maximum appearances of consent while assuring conformity. Sternness should be balanced with comradeliness and inexorable demands should be explained by superior knowledge. The party's monopoly is such that it is illicit even for a handful of people to meet regularly without a very good excuse, and all organizations must follow prescribed statutes and be specifically authorized by the competent authority. Even chess clubs and pensioners' recreational societies are subject to strict party control. It is assumed that in any organization there should be some party members, and these form a party fraction, which is responsible for the guidance of the organization.

The party also has control of personnel. Each party body has a list of positions in government and the economy for which it is responsible, to which it may name personnel or for which its assent is required. This list, the *nomenklatura*, is short for local bodies but includes many thousands of positions for higher; it is a vast field of patronage but it carries responsibility if nominees turn out badly. Party organizations are to keep their eye on other appointments, even though not on their own *nomenklatura.* Thus all important occupations, except some specialties, are tied practically into a single service. The party has almost complete control of the channels through which a Soviet citizen can advance himself materially or achieve anything of recognized significance.

Ordinary business goes through the departments attached to committees at all levels. These departments act as reporters, checkers, and means of liaison, allocating cadres, keeping dossiers, and inspecting compliance. They work with official and unofficial bodies at their own and inferior levels and with lower party bodies. At the lower levels, city and county *(raion)* or below, they are assisted by large numbers of volunteer and spare time inspectors, said to number over twenty-five million in 1971.

The sphere of party control is unbounded. Control of media or information is held of special importance; party committees at various levels have direct charge of leading newspapers and journals and give instructions to others. The writers and artists, among the least controllable elements of society, are also organized and directed. The party, not the intelligentsia, is critic of society and maker of morality. It watches over the selection of entrants to higher education, their instruction, and the administration of the schools; a party group may veto a university administrative decision. When boarding schools in Kirghizia are poorly organized, first the party and only secondarily the ministry are called upon to attend to them. Play needs party guidance; "Practice confirms the utility of party control over the plans for development of sports and their quality."[3] No field is too technical: "The party and the government pay great attention to the prevention of cancer . . ."[4]

The greatest preoccupation of the party, to judge from the volume of instructions, criticisms, and comments, is the overseeing of industry and agriculture. Party rules confer authority in productive enterprises: "Primary party organizations of industrial plants and trading establishments, state farms, collective farms, design and drafting agencies, and research institutes directly concerned with production have the right to control the work of the administration." The party secretary, although perhaps inconspicuous, seems to be the real boss in the factory. Not burdened with detail, he is in a better position to observe and criticize results. The party has most to say about personnel. If a boss has trouble with a subordinate, he will probably take it up not with the economic administration but with the party; if he comes into conflict with the party body at his level, he appeals, it would seem, to the next higher party body. Since the party controls, it cannot keep aloof from administration; and there has been a great deal of difficulty in determining where the line is to be drawn and how far the party is to go in ordering detail. The main emphasis, however, is on education, morale, non-material incentives, and organization of work.

In agriculture, the nominally elected, collective farm chairmen, are chosen by the party. The party secretary or the county instructor may have more to say about humdrum work assignments than the farm chairman; they have complete say-so as to the employment of party members. Party organizations in ministries and other central and local government departments should supervise, strengthen discipline, combat bureaucratism, observe and report on shortcomings, coordinate, select personnel, educate and indoctrinate, influence and advise, and cut red tape. The party enjoys the advantage of dealing with long-range and general affairs while remaining free of detailed administrative burdens, and it can control without being controlled. The party is frankly exempt from state law, but it makes law, "obliging" party and government workers to prescribed actions, sometimes mentioning its decrees as having full legal force. While ministries are often—sometimes bitterly —criticized, party organs are seldom objects of criticism and party policy is never subject to attack. All higher government officials are party members and so under party discipline, as are nearly all judges, army officers, and all or nearly all police.

Demarcation between party and government is indistinct. Top government officials have high party ranking, and high party leaders pronounce themselves freely on strictly governmental matters. The Central Committee approves the five year plan and "authorizes" the council of Ministers to proceed with it. There are joint party-state decrees at all levels; some enterprises formally pertain to both state and party, such as newspapers that are organs at once of the republican or regional central committee and the council of ministers. But the party is the only unified organization, and it seems clear that each ministry is more under the aegis of the corresponding department of the central committee than under that of the Council of Ministers. Ministries, like the army, the press, and the courts have no will or policy of their own in theory. Local party bodies are apt to control local government so closely as practically to take its place.

THE PARTY AND GROUP INTERESTS

The directing role of the party does not preclude the examination of other influences acting on or through the party to shape decision-making. The party is, to a certain extent, a representative body. People in all professions and categories belong to it; and they do not cease to be industrial managers, army officers, writers, or whatever their role in Soviet life may be when they acquire a party book. But the study of group tendencies in the Soviet Union, their divergence from the norm, and possible influence on the powers that be is difficult. Differing positions are expressed covertly and mildly, only in terms of different priorities and emphases. A trend may be berated in general ideological terms. No group can present itself frankly as a corporate entity seeking support or concessions for itself; all must represent themselves as expressing the public interest, of which the party is recognized guardian. It is hence a matter of judgment whether or to what extent one thinks of institutional groups (like the police), occupational categories (industrial managers or scientists), or agglomerations that may be formed over broad issues (like "liberals" or "hard-liners" in the Kremlin). Usually, merely personal followings are most evident, as are adherents of Brezhnev or Podgorny. Probably very few individuals are involved in whatever group pressures there may be, whether instigated by writers, jurists, managers, etc., because of the ban on recruiting support for group action.

In some ways, the party apparatus may stand in opposition to the state bureaucracy; perhaps in more ways divisions within the two sectors outweigh the division between them. At best, there are shadings of opinion and fluid alignments. If most writers on economics take the expectable position of favoring more freedom of managerial decision-making, others insist on the primacy of planning and party direction. The army is perhaps better prepared organizationally to form a coherent group, but the ground forces diverge from the rocket forces, the technicians from the line officers, and the political from the operational officers. The secret services have played an important part in the past and may, for all the outside world knows, have a large role in policy formation behind the scenes today. There is apparently rivalry between the civilian security forces (KGB) and military intelligence. The most influential must be those whose work is close to that of the party, the military, heads of government departments, trade-unions, Komsomol and such semipolitical organizations, and managers of major industries.

Institutions or groups obviously look to their own interests. It appears that the profitability of tobacco and alcoholic beverages has a good deal to do with their continued large-scale use in the Soviet Union as in the United States, although party policy opposes them. When youth cafes were set up in 1961 to get young people off the streets, the Ministry of Trade turned them into liquor outlets for commercial reasons and defeated the idea. There has apparently been disagreement between those interested in electric power and those concerned with the flooding of useful land by hydroelectric projects; at least, the ministers of power and agriculture stressed opposite sides of the question in speeches at the Twenty-Fourth Congress.

It is reasonable to assume that when party bodies make policies, they take into account who is for and who is against. The party at the same time wishes to see no other body or group in a position to exert political pressure contrary to party policy. By its penetration of and direction of all organizations and particularly by its control of staffing through the *nomenklatura,* it imposes the fusion of contrary interests. Experts and specialists play an increasing role in the modernizing Soviet economy and have in recent years been able to speak out on issues of public policy concerning which the party has no fixed position. But outsiders have authority rather because they are valuable than because they have autonomous power. Their relation to the party is a little like that of a man who wishes to build a home to his architect. The builder picks the professional, sets the specifications, and heeds or disregards his recommendations as he will. But because he wants a proper house, much decision-making necessarily rests with the expert. Moreover, the builder knows that his architect will work better if he is treated with consideration and heard with attention even though his recommendations may not be fully accepted.

If the evolution of the Soviet state proceeds like that of other authoritarian systems, it is likely that the ability of the center to reach and enforce decisions will decline gradually, even apart from the complicating effects of technology. The apparatus grows stiffer and less responsive; vested interests learn, openly or covertly, to defend themselves. The party, with less dynamic will of its own, becomes more of a mediator and aggregator of different interests, speaking less for itself and more for others who speak through it. But the divergences emerging in Soviet society may at best be comparable to the self-will of various departments within the government of the United States; few sectors of the Soviet system are as independent of the Politburo as the State Department is of the American president who is legally its master.

No political structure, however despotic, is really monolithic. There are always conflicting wills behind the scenes. The despot rarely sees his orders carried out in quite the way he would like, and is always dependent upon his apparatus, often at its mercy. Under the tyranny usually recalled as the model of totalitarianism, Hitler's Third Reich, there was much more evidence of group autonomy than in the Soviet Union today. Elite groups contested bitterly, while Hitler acted as supreme arbiter, seldom trying to overrule the majority of his inferiors.

Like any political system, the Soviet must reconcile and adjudicate a multitude of interests. The most remarkable political fact about the

Soviet system is the degree to which Lenin's party has been able, by purposeful organization and ideological commitment, to centralize basic policy direction of a huge and diverse modern country and to minimize the ability of any group to press for its own policies. "It would be a profound mistake to suppose that such exceptional harmony in the coordination of different complex aspects of social existence, which any bourgeois government might envy, comes of itself. It is the result of the titanic organizational work of the Communist party, based on the great ideas of Marxism-Leninism."[5] Much depends upon how effectively it can maintain the present degree of harmony.

FOOTNOTES

1. *Pravda*, December 19, 1969.
2. *ibid*, January 11, 1970.
3. *ibid*, November 16, 1969.
4. *ibid*, September 3, 1969.
5. A. Aimbetov, M. Baimakonov, and M. Imashev, *Problemy sovershenstvovaniia organizatsii i deiatelnosti mestnykh sovetov* (Izd. Nauka, Alma Ata, 1967), p. 87.

CHAPTER 8

The Government

The Soviet government is not clearly bounded. It includes the apparatus of civilian order, the power which conducts foreign relations and defense, makes rules and punishes for their infraction, and carries on through ministries and departments of state the functions ordinarily filled by governments. However, the chief business of the Soviet government is administration of the economy, which is managed separately. The armed forces, security police, courts, economic ministries, etc., are tied together by little more than common responsibility to the party. The system of pseudolegislative bodies, the soviets, forms a separate branch which intermeshes with the administration to some extent, especially on the local level, but which is another instrument of the party. Party and government-administrative spheres overlap; and various other organizations, such as the trade-unions and Komsomol, perform official duties. The former administer the social security system. It is likewise unclear where a line can be drawn between party policy and regular law.

The revolutionaries of 1917 assumed that they came not to reform the state but to abolish it. While they had to have a government, they claimed that theirs was essentially different from that of earlier states because of its "class content." Its theoretical basis was the system of more or less proletarian councils, in Russian "soviets," which sprang up in the vacuum caused by the collapse of tsardom. Lenin envisioned working people gathering briefly to vote on the right course of action and going back to their jobs. This would imply leaving the real business of government to men who were in a position to devote full time to it. From the very first, an executive committee took over most of the business of the Petrograd Soviet and an inner circle took over the direction of the executive committee. The Congress of Soviets to which Lenin handed power was sent home after endorsement of the new regime and its initial proclamations. Subsequently, as the Soviet government gained strength, it reduced the powers of soviets, local and regional as well as central, to the point of triviality or fiction. It also looked very much as if the old bureaucratic apparatus had revived, with ministries (named "commissariats" until after the Second World War), secret police, and centralized administration. The soviets remained, however, the formal basis for equating the will of the party with the will of the masses, the legitimating foundation for an amorphous administrative structure.

CONSTITUTION

To formalize structures, a constitution was provided for the Russian territories in 1918 and for the Soviet Union in 1923. In 1936, as Stalin was nearing the completion of his transformation of Soviet society and the consolidation of his absolutism, he had drawn up a new document reflecting, it was stated, the advances toward socialism; but this contained few important changes. Despite talk of its replacement, it is still in effect.

In Marxist thinking, a constitution cannot really limit the power of the ruling classes. In this light, the Soviet constitution reflects the principles of "dictatorship of the proletariat," proclaiming popular government without restraining the ruling power. It provides a complete framework for democratic government, with parliamentary bodies elected by universal secret ballot, governments responsible to these, and an impressive set of rights. The latter include freedom of speech and the press, inviolability of persons and of the home, and the like. Not merely "bourgeois" liberties are guaranteed; Soviet citizens have a constitutional right to work, to leisure, to maintenance in case of need, and to education. The right to freedom of the press is to be made effective for the masses by "placing at the disposal of the working people and their organizations printing presses, stocks of paper, public buildings, the streets, communications facilities and other material requisites for the exercise of these rights" (Article 125). This constitution was used to cast Stalin in the role of a great democrat, and many persons not only in Russia but abroad saw it as a statement of excellent intentions if not an actual realization of liberty and equality. It was rather widely assumed that the right of public organizations to nominate candidates was seriously intended and thus that there would be freely contested elections, unknown in Soviet practice since 1917.

But there is no means for a citizen to sue for observance of promised rights, and no means for any assertion of independence from the party. Political rights are for party-controlled organizations only. The constitution is not cited judicially and is easily amendable. Despite this, the government has several times acted contrary to it, only later making the requisite amendments. Some provisions are purely propagandistic, as the unequivocal statement of the right of Soviet republics to secede (Article 17), any attempt to exercise which would be treason. It might be said that the real constitution of the USSR is the well-understood supremacy of the party.

ELECTIONS

Elections are held every four years for supreme soviets (of the Soviet Union and constituent republics), every two years for local soviets. Much is made over the equality of the franchise for races, sexes, and nationalities and of its universality; no Western nation can boast of participation approaching 100% as can the Soviet Union. Soviet elections are exemplary in all ways except in failure to permit an election, that is, a choice.

There is no legal reason that there should not be real contests, and the instructions on the ballot imply a plurality of candidates: "Leave on the ballot paper the name of ONE candidate for whom you vote, cross out the remainder." But party authorities at each level decide whom to nominate in the single-member districts. The candidate is then presented to a nomination meeting of some organization, like a trade-union, perhaps open to the public. This is a festive affair, and the nomination and all motions related to it are normally approved unanimously. It is possible on some occasions, especially in villages, that the suggested candidate proves so unpopular that he is withdrawn. The electoral commissions are authorized to exclude candidates but have not had to exercise the power.

Probably the party tries to choose, as it says, "the best people," in the sense of getting men devoted to the cause, respected by their fellows, and qualified to carry out their duties of assisting mobilization, leadership, and relations with the public. Nomination is also an honor and reward for good work. Along with a few exemplary workers and farmers, persons of influence and importance are nominated, including party workers, managers, commanders of the local garrison and of the police. About half of the two million deputies nominated at each election time are new.

It would seem that, since the party controls nominations, it might well permit two or more trusted individuals to contest the election. This would make it vastly more interesting, would be a challenge to the candidates, and would greatly improve the image of the Soviet Union. The evident reason for not doing so is fear of the entering wedge of division. If two candidates began vying for support, it would be difficult to prevent their touching upon real issues and exposing fissures in the Soviet society.

After nomination there are about two months of meetings, speeches, and exhortations, not for the benefit of the individual candidate but of the Soviet system, with praise of "socialist democracy" as against "bourgeois" elections, which are allegedly controlled by capitalists and marked by bribery, intimidation, and discrimination.

Everyone must vote, although the obligation is unofficial, and according to the record only one in two hundred fails to do so. Electoral helpers rouse people from their apartments and carry ballot boxes to the hospitals. Travellers passing through vote as residents. Contumacious refusal to participate may be cause for banishment. There are no write-ins, and the voter need not mark the ballot but merely put it in the box. To cast a negative vote is rather conspicuous.

Despite this, from one to four voters per thousand vote against the official candidates according to Soviet figures. Voters in small villages and settlements may have some power to make themselves felt. To be counted elected, a candidate must receive a majority of favorable ballots. Roughly one twenty-thousandth of local candidates may be announced defeated after elections.

Elections furnish "a powerful demonstration of the monolithic unity of the Communist party and the people."[1] The campaigns are an occasion for propaganda and political involvement. It is desirable that all citizens engage in a symbolic act of support for the Soviet government, even though this is as slight as giving token assent by dropping a piece of paper in a box. The elections also serve propagandistic purposes abroad, along with the rights declared by the constitution, and the pseudoparliamentary institutions. Conforming to model democratic patterns in many ways, they influence not only the naive but many intelligent persons.

The elections may also be fairly convincing for Soviet citizens. In capitalist countries, they are told, the ordinary people have no means of putting forward their candidates, but in the Soviet Union the union nominates a good worker to the high legislative body. The people know very little of democracy; government is exalted and to be consulted is a concession. Long indoctrinated with the necessity of unity, they are apt to regard the idea of competing parties with repugnance. Soviet press reports of successes of Communist parties under capitalist tyranny may make the Soviet variety of elections seem a humiliating comedy to some of the educated; but elections are part of the apparatus of the modern state, from which the Russians have borrowed appearances, and they cannot easily be renounced.

THE SUPREME SOVIET

The Great Hall of the Kremlin is host twice yearly, for about ten days, to a colorful assembly of about fifteen hundred Kirghiz herders, Ukrainian tractor drivers, Baltic factory workers, and their counterparts from all over Russia, along with staid managers and party secretaries. In a bow to the federal pattern of Soviet administration, the Supreme Soviet is divided into two chambers. In the Soviet of the Union, seats are allocated on the basis of population; the other, the Soviet of Nationalities, is composed of deputies from union republics, "autonomous republics," "autonomous regions," and "national areas." In theory, the deputy is to be legislator and controller of the government (he has no office and no staff) and to carry the laws to the people while holding a full time job. A majority of deputies are new at each election, as the reward is passed out to the deserving; the body has little continuity.

The Supreme Soviet formally approves the ministry, ratifies laws and decrees issued in its absence, passes a few laws, and approves the state budget and economic plan. Most time in session (about four hours daily in two yearly sessions totalling three to five days on the average) is given to hearing official reports. Deputies also report on the progress of their constituencies, praise the government's proposals, and sometimes suggest minor changes. Speeches of deputies, usually two to five minutes in length, are practically indistinguishable in style and substance. Votes, which are open, are always unanimous, no abstentions having been recorded. In 1955, the resignation of Malenkov was sprung as a surprise but the deputies unanimously approved it without discussion.

The standing of the Supreme Soviet has varied slightly. It was much in the shadows during Stalin's last years, meeting briefly and seldom. In the later Khrushchev years, there was some limited questioning from the floor of the assembly, and the "standing commissions" of the Supreme Soviet seemed slightly more active. However, recent years have seen a retreat both in the length of sessions and the latitude permitted the deputies. The Supreme Soviet nonetheless affords desk-bound Moscow leaders an opportunity to meet and talk with persons from many walks of life and all parts of the country. Having been honored and educated, they are to carry the word back to the grass roots. It is also useful to give certain laws, especially those touching very many people, such as that of military training, the sanctity of passage by the Supreme Soviet. This body thus serves like the tsarist Council of State to solemnly register decrees.

The other obvious purpose of the Supreme Soviet is to serve as democratic facade. It is much reported and photographed, and is freely referred to by non-Communists as well as Communists as the "Soviet Parliament" (despite Lenin's vehement rejection of parliamentary government). It is doubtless necessary to have something like the Supreme Soviet as window-dressing. "Our parliament is much more democratic than the American Congress," ordinary Soviet citizens repeat, "because in the Congress there are no farmers or workers."

THE PRESIDIUM

The Presidium of the Supreme Soviet is theoretically an elected presiding committee of that assembly but in fact is a practically separate organ. By the constitution it possesses most of the powers of the Supreme Soviet during the 98% of the time that the latter is not in session; that is, it passes laws, approves ministers, and the like. The greater part of the published acts of the Presidium consists of the granting of honors and the making of diplomatic appointments. When, where, or whether it really meets remains a mystery.

The president of the Presidium is the formal head of the Soviet state. Formerly the post was purely decorative, its duties being largely handing out medals and receiving foreign ambassadors. It has recently seemed to become more significant, as Podgorny has been given second place in the Soviet ranking order; but how he exercises political power is obscure. Possibly it has been upgraded in order to split prestige with the chairman of the Council of Ministers, whose administrative responsibilities furnish a potentially more solid power base.

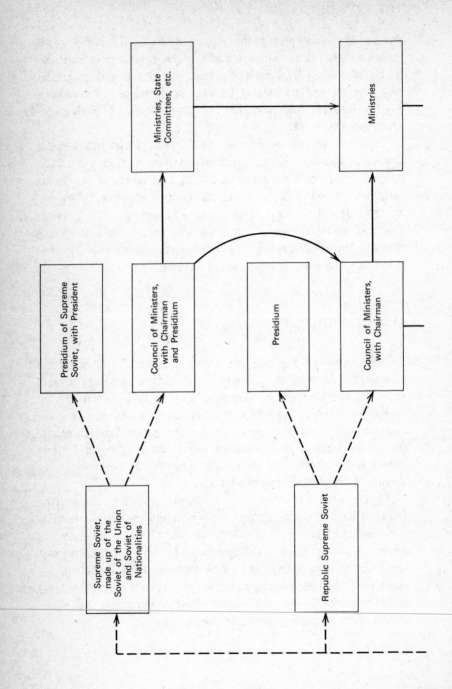

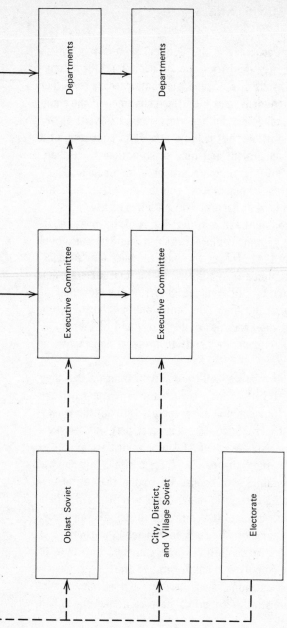

Simplified outline of governmental structure. Dotted lines signify formal election or right of approval. Solid lines signify administrative authority. At each level, governmental organs are under corresponding party organizations.

THE COUNCIL OF MINISTERS

The top of the state bureaucracy is the Council of Ministers, which includes heads of about fifty ministries, mostly economic (the number has fluctuated greatly), heads of a dozen state committees, a few other government agencies or councils, and the fifteen chairmen of the councils of ministers of the republics. Perhaps this group of about eighty persons never meets as a whole; but it has a presidium consisting of a chairman, two first vice-chairmen, and nine or so ordinary vice-chairmen. The Council of Ministers, or more probably its presidium, may serve as something of an administrative coordinator. It is also the principal Soviet issuer of laws or decrees with the force of law.

The presidency of the Council of Ministers is one of the most important posts in the Soviet system. Lenin occupied it and Stalin assumed it as clouds gathered in 1941. It was the base for Malenkov's leadership, and Khrushchev occupied it in addition to the first secretaryship as soon as he was able to do so in 1958. After the downfall of Khrushchev, it was resolved by the party center and sanctioned by the Central Committee that the headships of the party and of the administration should be kept in separate hands to preserve collectivity of leadership.

About half of the ministries are "All-Union," which means that they operate throughout the USSR in their own name. The other half are "Union-Republic," which means that they operate through the corresponding ministries of the republics. For the most part, matters best handled at the All-Union level are under All-Union ministries, as are the Merchant Marine and defense industry. But foreign affairs and defense are nominally Union-Republic as a concession to the theoretical sovereignty of the republics, although in reality totally centralized. There are dual lines of control: from central ministry to republic ministries and from the USSR Council of Ministers to the republic councils of ministers, while innumerable committees and councils contribute to making the world's most complicated administrative setup.

The apparatus under the ministers is hardly a bureaucracy in the classic sense. The administrative superiors have restricted control of appointments and promotions, which are concerns of the party. There are no regularized career ladders with rules for advancement; there is no formal security of tenure, although bureaucrats in practice hold their places for long periods, and Soviet press accounts indicate that officials strongly protect one another. Lines of authority are multiple and often confused, to judge from complaints of evasion of responsibility. One may surmise that coordination within the governmental maze is to a large extent informal and that decisions are reached by irregular consultation and personal contact.

FEDERAL STRUCTURE

Efficiency demands some devolution of administration, and ethnic divisions of the USSR are the primary units for this purpose. The fifteen "republics" came to exist largely from the historical process of bringing back under the sway of Moscow the peoples who had broken away during the period of weakness after the revolution. There are also twenty "autonomous republics" which do not enjoy trappings of sovereignty, sixteen of them within the huge Russian republic. Their autonomy consists chiefly in legal use of the minority language.

Much is made of the sovereignty of the union republics; in practice, however, the republics are only administrative subdivisions. Their constitutions follow closely that of the union and are essentially identical, even in wording. The chief differences are that some provide for different subdivisions or ministries according to local need, such as a ministry of cotton production in Uzbekistan. No field of importance is left to republic jurisdiction, and the republics have practical rights only as convenient to the central authorities.

Nonetheless, a good deal of the process of government seems to go forward at the republic level. Practical and local details are written into the framework of All-Union laws, and policies may be implemented at a different tempo in the various republics, which fill in the specifics of budgets handed to them from the center. They also have legal responsibility for the local governments beneath them.

LOCAL SOVIETS

Each administrative layer has its popular-representative legitimating soviet. The supreme soviets of the republics are much like the All-Union Supreme Soviet, large acclamatory bodies. Lower on the scale, the soviets decrease in size and meet oftener. Regional soviets are obliged to meet at least four times yearly, those at the bottom level six times. Apparently they often fail to comply with these requirements, however, and the sessions are likely to be one day or less.

This inactivity reflects the lack of autonomy of the soviets. Party leadership is absolute. Officers of the soviets generally seem to be named from outside, and they are frequently not even members of the soviets over which they preside. The soviets have jurisdiction only over matters that no higher body cares to handle, and have no funds at their discretion but only small allotments from above. The meetings, which are closed to the public, tend to be formal; the conventional pattern is like that of party meetings, and the agenda consists of taking note of successes, conceding shortcomings, and promising remedies. The main occupation of deputies is carrying on relations with the people, mobilizing them, and binding them closer to the Soviet government. Deputies hold office hours to hear petitioners, investigate social and personal problems, and act as all-around propagandists, helping to make the new Soviet man.

The local soviets serve a semigovernmental function as the principal focus for the organization of volunteer and semivolunteer activities. All manner of groups for civic purposes, mostly for control, are organized under their auspices. There are apartment committees, street committees, borough or ward committees, parents' groups, and hospital councils. Probably most important are the "standing commissions" of the soviets, in which deputies are joined by outside activists in more or less equal numbers; this is also a means of associating persons of special or technical qualifications with the work of the soviets. The commissions, of which there are more than three hundred thousand, deal with such matters as education, the militia (ordinary police), health, transportation, housing, juvenile affairs, parks, and retail trade, working with and supplementing the regular local administrative apparatus. A total of twenty-three million activists are said to cooperate with local soviets in various ways.[2]

LOCAL ADMINISTRATION

The Petrograd Soviet of 1917 permitted decision-making to fall to an inner group called the "executive committee," and the center of soviet local administration at all levels below the republic is so designated. Theoretically an emanation of the elected soviet, the executive committee is actually a different body, a part not of the soviet but of the administrative apparatus. It is a cabinet of paid state officials, probably about a dozen in small cities, twice as many in larger. Around the executive committees, with departments like ministries, there is a proliferation of agencies. Party and government bodies are often inseparably intermingled in personnel and functions.

The field of local government includes everything higher authorities prefer not to handle directly, such as local transportation, services, retail trade, school, and perhaps housing, although this is more likely to be associated with industrial enterprises. The local administration serves as coordinator of collective farms, local industry, and cultural institutions even though these are subordinate to other agencies. But it can initiate practically nothing without superior authorization. Heads of city departments are not merely checked by the respective ministry but are named and dismissed by it.

DEMOCRACY AND DICTATORSHIP

The Soviet problem is to sustain and make workable a strong rulership without traditional basis in an age of democracy and nationalistic and individualistic self-assertion. This has required ideology and indoctrination, with a party monopoly of information. It is necessary for the powers that be, however, not merely to repeat endlessly that the Soviet Union is a people's state which the people must obey and support, but to give it appearances of popular government.

The Soviet is skilled in using democratic forms to strengthen the authority of a ruling elite. Democratic appearances help to suppress criticism as "anti-popular," and the official preemption of the vocabulary of rights and freedom psychologically disarms the opposition. As long as the party monopoly of information and organization remains absolute, any small overt steps in the democratic direction may be designed further to affirm party rule. It is a major advantage of the formal separation of party and state that democratic and constitutional appearances can be introduced into what is called the "government" without blemishing the monopoly of power in the governing party.

The Soviet rulership is nonetheless very cautious. Thus they decline to make the use of elections and soviets that would seem at first sight quite feasible. To make legitimate any political contest would require drawing up effective rules for the allocation of power; this might prove dangerous for the monopoly of the center because of the contradictions of pretenses and reality. Discussion of issues is nearly excluded. Public "debates," as of the Party Program in 1961, have been kept within narrow limits and have had no obvious relation to decisions taken. Since Khrushchev, public airing even of undecided issues has been further narrowed.

To avoid open controversy and to veil the gap between front and inner substance, the workings of the system are thoroughly shrouded in secrecy. There is no public weighing of the merits of anyone in an important position; it is not even felt necessary to give explanations of promotions or demotions, unless the individual is to be used as an example. Lines of real command are hidden; the citizen is told nothing, for example, of the departments of the Central Committee and their responsibilities. Practically everything to do with policy-making is concealed, so that if a debate is publicized it is not important. To divulge divisions of any kind would raise questions as to the infallibility of the leadership and would also encourage many persons to believe that they might have a claim to influence the decision. Secrecy hence becomes a principle. Not only is it impossible for Soviet writers to analyze issues or personalities in politics; they cannot even write critically of the mechanics of government. But the separation of rulers from ruled makes for apathy and cynicism; the uninformed are indifferent.

The Soviet commitment to democratic forms is equivocal. The Soviet Encyclopedic Dictionary (1963) defines democracy as "The form of government in which the will of the majority is legally recognized as the basis of authority, and freedom and equality of citizens are proclaimed." Democracy is thus treated as a matter of formal recognition and proclamation of freedom and equality. In other connections, democracy is defined primarily in terms of social rights, people's ownership of the economy, and above all, citizens' participation in the execution of policy. The more persons mobilized, the more popular the government.

In *What is to Be Done* Lenin wrote that "broad democracy" in Russian conditions was only a *"useless and harmful toy"*[3] (Lenin's emphasis), a remarkable statement in view of the usual readiness of those out of power to subscribe to democratic rights. Brezhnev quoted Lenin at the June, 1969, Congress of Communist Parties: "'Pure democracy' is a deceitful liberal phrase to make fools of the workers."[4] Soviet writers do not hesitate to decry "arithmetic" or "mechanical" majorities when votes go contrary to their purposes, and to speak of the necessary "dictatorship of the proletariat" even while claiming the most democratic of governments.

The essence of the Soviet way is "consciousness" over "spontaneity," to use the terms of Lenin nearly seventy years ago. There is little room for separate individual or group urges apart from the ideals of the system or the purposes of those who stand at its head. "Discipline is one of the unvarying conditions of democracy. The requirements of discipline are deeply democratic, because they assure unity of will for the attainment of the common goal, the successful functioning of the state."[5] The leit-motif and theme is always unity.

FOOTNOTES

1. *Partinaia zhizn,* no. 3, February, 1969.
2. *Pravda,* December 5, 1969.
3. *Collected Works,* vol. 5 (Moscow, 1961), p. 479.
4. *Pravda,* June 8, 1969.
5. *Nauchnye osnovy gosudarstvennogo upravleniia v SSSR,* (Akad. Nauk, Moscow, 1968) p. 418.

CHAPTER 9

The Military

The Soviet system rests on several pillars: its ideological justification, the party incorporating the political will, and the governmental apparatus administering and mobilizing. To these must be added the military establishment as ultimate guarantor of the system—a firm backstop for ideology, party, and government. It is the servant and ally of the ruling elite, but is also a threat to them, the visible alternative political power. In nonconstitutional states, the possessors of physical force are inevitably politically powerful, perhaps in quiet ways but decisively so in crisis or threatened breakdown.

Thus far, however, the Soviet leadership has been remarkably successful in checking what they have always feared: military takeover of their state. Their first urge was to do away with the military forces altogether. Having had to put together a large army in the civil war, the leaders sufficiently infused it with revolutionary spirit and controlled it through the Bolshevik commissars that it played no consequential political role. From the end of the civil war to the mid-1930's, the army was kept relatively small. It then began a steady buildup, but Stalin so battered the officer corps in the purges that it displayed no self-will during the Second World War or as long as Stalin lived.

After his departure, the role of the military became more prominent, although it remains difficult to assess. Glorification of the armed forces

137

in the Soviet press has increased, especially since Khrushchev; they are second only to the party. As the Soviet state becomes more conservative, their role almost inevitably rises. They not only have the physical force to take control whenever they might resolve to do so; they have coherence and a unified command unmatched by no other Soviet sector except the party itself. There is no real constitutional or ideological bar to their undertaking to remove what they might consider a defective leadership or insisting on political changes for the safety of the land. It cannot be excluded that, by sudden shift or slow evolution, the old Bolshevik fear of a Bonapartist turn may yet be realized, bringing the Soviet Union, like China, nearer the patterns of outright military dictatorship so common in the world.

THE PARTY IN THE MILITARY

To forestall this possibility, the party leadership has always taken great pains to extend its own apparatus into the army and to keep a close check on the military establishment in every possible way. The party has also sought to indoctrinate soldiers and officers in the necessity of absolute obedience to it, much as any army indoctrinates its men in absolute obedience to the command structure. The party has made itself the supreme military commander with its special lines of authority into every military unit.

One arm of the party's apparatus of control is the security police under the KGB, with agents at the regimental staff level and above. It has regular army ranks and uniform but operates under its own command structure. Security officers are concerned with morale and anti-Soviet feelings, as well as with counterespionage. They also check on the work of military and political officers, keep dossiers and pass on promotions.

Control is also effected through party and Komsomol organization. Recruits are pressed to join the Komsomol, and about four-fifths of the men in the ranks belong. Virtually all officers are party or Komsomol members. The party organization in the army differs from that in civilian life in that its head is not the nominally elected secretary but the appointed political officer of the unit. The political officer, "zampolit," belongs to the hierarchy of the Chief Political Administration, a department of the Central Committee, with a chain of command parallel to that of the army from top to bottom.

The zampolit is descendant of the commissars, reliable Bolsheviks set to watch tsarist officers recruited for expertise in the civil war but feared because of their background. He remains primarily a morale officer, working mostly through the party group and the party members, who, including the commander, are subordinate to him as party leader and whose promotions depend on his reports along with those of the KGB representative. He is chaplain, educator, censor, and instructor. With a staff of officers, including full-time propagandists and secretaries of party and Komsomol committees, he provides daily instruction on foreign and domestic affairs and party policy, obligatory for all enlisted personnel. There are lectures, numerous to the point of interfering with military duties, discussion groups, indoctrination movies, ratio and television programs. Above all, the political educators must work by personal agitation, in which the officer, like a father, helps resolve personal problems and build character, molding soldiers into warriors totally inspired and obedient, completely immune to "bourgeois" ideology, vigilant against hostile infiltration, and ever mindful of their "patriotic and international duty."

Since 1956 the political apparatus has been responsible not only for political but for general military training. The zampolit helps teach men how to handle tanks while he is inculcating their Soviet-patriotic and proletarian-internationalist duty, and the party apparatus concerns itself with general policies, personnel questions, and technical aspects of military assignments. The commander himself is supposed to undergo self-criticism at party meetings and may be called upon to justify his professional competence. Although his orders are not to be criticized, the party may sit in judgment over his treatment of subordinates.

THE MILITARY IN SOVIET SOCIETY

If the party permeates the armed forces, the military has tentacles throughout Soviet society. The party indoctrinates the army, but the army in turn indoctrinates the people, while every effort is made to prevent the exclusiveness which is characteristic of military establishments of other countries. Over a score of top commanders are members of the Central Committee, and military men participate in party leadership in the oblasts or republics. At a lower level, party rules require that party bodies in the forces "maintain close contact with local party committees and keep them informed concerning political activities within the military units. Secretaries of military party organizations and heads of political bodies participate in the work of local party committees." Many officers are deputies in local soviets. Military party groups are to work with factories and farms of the area where they may be stationed, telling the workers of the successes of the warriors, hearing tell, in turn, of the victories of workers and farmers, and helping to cultivate love for the army and navy among the people, especially the youth.

Military service (ordinarily two years, longer in special branches, and one year for persons with higher education) is not a mere interlude but an integral part of the life of the Soviet male. A part of entry into manhood, it ideally transforms the raw youth into a modest but self-assured, strong, self-sacrificing, disciplined Soviet citizen. On the solemn induction day, for which they should ideologically prepare themselves, the new recruits are welcomed by veterans, hear inspiring speeches and stirring music, and take the military oath in the presence of the assembled citizenry, surrounded by banners and mementoes of dead heroes. A man's eyes take on a new glow, as his factory stops work to give its draftees a proper send-off.

The draftee has had ample opportunity through boyhood to absorb military spirit and the ways of the soldier. From preschool age, he was encouraged to play war games. As Pioneers, children engage in an endless round of semimilitary ceremonies with accents on struggle and brotherhood, and learn to rout the enemy with toy automatics.

Children's magazines are filled with military-patriotic themes. Schools have military museums, sponsor countless excursions to places of glory, and receive visits of veterans and heroes.

Civil defense lessons begin with the fifth grade. Formal, obligatory military training is supposed to begin after the eighth grade, whether the boy continues in secondary school or goes to work. It is conducted by the army, which details officers on active duty or reserve officers to act as instructors. The Soviet paramilitary defense organization, Dosaaf works with the Komsomol. Students in higher education also must pass military courses throughout their university careers. Otherwise they are subject to draft as privates instead of qualifying for officer status upon graduation.

The name of Dosaaf is composed of the Russian initials for "Voluntary Society for Cooperation with the Army, Air Force, and Fleet." With a membership of over forty million, it is one of the great organizations of Soviet society and an important link with the masses. Its structure parallels that of the party; and party, trade-union, economic, and especially Komsomol organizations are obliged to cooperate with it. With branches in factories, farms, and higher schools, Dosaaf carries on civil defense instruction and trains in military skills and sports, teaching especially such sports as motorcycle riding, fencing, marksmanship, grenade throwing, and obstacle racing. It trains a million or so technical specialists yearly.

There are many other forms of indoctrination. Factories have their military instruction sections, probably under a reserve officer, for firing practice and other exercises as well as for general morale and the fostering of the "military and revolutionary traditions" of the Soviet people. Millions of boys and girls are taken on pilgrimages to the innumerable war monuments and shrines which hallow battles of the civil war and the Great Patriotic War, where they dedicate themselves equally to serve the Soviet fatherland. Outstanding military heroes are kept busy addressing groups, especially of school children, and participating in ceremonies; they hand out to sixteen-year-olds the passports which attest their citizenship. The county (raion) should have its patriotic museum of "military and labor glory" and hold regular sessions at which veterans speak of the "heroic traditions of party and people." In the past several years the life of the army and its past glories, especially in the Second World War, have been made subject of a flood of writing and movies. Military themes are perennial in all media, particularly newspapers, books, and television, in tales and reminiscences, accounts of training exercises and the day-to-day duties of soldiers. The ever-alert border guards and dramas of successes in battling the enemy are especially popular themes.[*]

The Soviet soldier is both the bearer of proletarian internationalism and heir to the glories of Russian armies of ages past. Russian nationalism is tied to Soviet Marxist supranationalism, and medieval battles are interpreted both as Russians against Germans or Mongols and as the people against would-be enslavers. Nothing may detract from the heroic aura. Presumably for this reason, no statistics of war losses have been published. When feeble tendencies toward realistic portrayal of war appeared in the years of maximum relaxation of the early 1960's, they were firmly put down as sordid and unpatriotic.

THE MILITARY ECONOMY

Announced Soviet military appropriations, recently somewhat over seventeen billion rubles, are modest for such a large country. But this figure tells little. Military training is charged to education; research and development can be covered by appropriations for science and heavy industry; Aeroflot provides services for the air force. Manpower

[*]"What a word, 'soldier'! In its very rhythm one hears the precise cadence of the parade march, and the iron roar of winds at the front, and the victorious, ancient, yet new Russian 'Hurrah!' But not only that. We say, 'Soldier of the Fatherland' and we see before us a man of high goals and lofty duty, a man of generous spirit and warm challenging heart. With the word 'soldier' are indissolubly bound concepts of valor, faithfulness, discipline, and friendship, pure as a mountain spring, hard as adamant . . ." (Kazakhstanskaia pravda, February 18, 1971.)

is paid at subsistence cost, as soldiers receive only trivial pocket money (partly to spare them the temptation of vodka). Procurement prices are very low; much or most of the cost is shifted to the producer. A ruble spent by the armed forces may have ten or even twenty times the purchasing power of a ruble in the hands of a consumer.

Soviet military expenditures can thus be best estimated by the results. The Soviet Union maintains armed forces substantially larger than those of the United States and equips them with weapons universally rated as first quality, in many cases the world's best. It has a great variety of advanced planes and develops new ones. Soviet military transport showed great efficiency in the 1968 airborne invasion of Czechoslovakia. The Soviet navy, which Khrushchev downgraded, has been rapidly expanded to a world-girdling force with indefinite perspectives, comparable to the American except in aircraft carriers, and much newer. The Soviet submarine fleet is by far the world's largest. From 1965 to 1971, while the number of American intercontinental missiles rose only slightly, the Soviet force increased fivefold to about 1600, against 1054 on the American side. The explosive power of the Soviet weapons, moreover, is several times larger than the American, so total Soviet megatonnage is reportedly several times larger than that of the United States.

Such a military buildup represents a burden for an economy approximately half the size of the American; in other words, it may be roughly estimated that the military component of the Soviet economy is proportionately about double that of the American. The Soviet economy has been oriented to heavy industry since the First Five-Year Plan; and heavy industry has served primarily to create the foundations not of consumer goods production but of military production. Military and industrial management are also closely associated. The armed forces have special schools to qualify officers in the technology of various branches of production, such as aircraft, chemical, and artillery; and officers are attached to heavy industrial enterprises to expedite military production and coordinate mobilization planning. Soviet lead times in weapons development have been consistently shorter than American and the quality and imaginativeness of Soviet military goods has contrasted with that of civilian goods.

THE MILITARY AND THE PARTY

Because of the fading of revolutionary spirit and the decline of dynamism of the civilian leadership, it is not surprising that military influence should grow as the Soviet Union matures. After the Second World War, Stalin tried to check the military leadership by scattering the most outstanding marshals. However, the relative decline of the party as an instrument of rule in Stalin's last years gave them increased importance, as shown by the fact that nearly all the alleged victims of the Doctors' Plot were military. After the death of the dictator, the party needed army support against Beria's police. The execution of the latter and the reduction of the power of the security forces benefited the military element as much as the party. De-Stalinization came to dilute the generals' respect for the party's infallibility. In 1957, the army played a decisive part in Khrushchev's victory.

Marshal Zhukov thereby earned promotion from candidate (which he had become a few months earlier) to full member of the Presidium (Politburo) of the party, the first real military figure to enjoy this station. If he had remained, the army might have staked out a prominent place at the political summit. But Khrushchev expelled him both from the Presidium and from the post of Minister of Defense in October-November, 1957. Zhukov's most obvious sin was being too powerful, but he was accused of seeking personal glory, and it was inferred that he had sought to seize power.

As a result of the crisis, the party moved to strengthen the role of the political officers and to broaden their responsibilities. But the place of the military in the Soviet political picture expanded as the authority of Khrushchev became less firm after 1960 and particularly after the humiliation of the Cuban crisis in 1962. The generals became apprehensive of Khrushchev's consumerism and protested his efforts to reduce the size of the forces; they exerted pressure against these measures and for heavy industry and defense spending.

The ouster of the innovative chairman represented a victory for the conservative-military point of view. The fading of utopianism and the failure of Khrushchev's hopes for victory in economic competition made it logical that greater reliance should be placed in the army, the readiest antidote for liberalization. The military demonstrated its usefulness in foreign affairs in the Arab world and in Eastern Europe. In 1967 it was reported that the marshals had rejected a nonmilitary candidate favored by a majority of the Politburo for the position of Minister of Defense and secured the nomination of one of their own, Marshal Grechko. The latter became prominent as an executor of Soviet policy in relations with countries of the Soviet sphere. The military role in education was enlarged and the military view prevailed in literature.

The Soviet leadership wishes to use the military, not to share power with them. However, the party and the army are not so much separate and potentially opposed institutions as they are different aspects of the basic Soviet pattern. The militant party itself is not far from a military organization. Despite its concessions to consultation below, it is, like armies everywhere, elitist and hierarchic. Its principles of obedience are stern. Discipline is its watchword in the everlasting war against the class enemy. In the civil war, the party was practically an army, and members were subject to assignment to whatever duty deemed most necessary. Military terminology has continued to flavor the party's language: peasants celebrate their "victory" in the "battle" to harvest the hay, and "fighting" ("boevoi"), with numerous derivatives, is one of the commonest terms of the Soviet vocabulary. The extensive use of uniforms and decorations is in the same spirit.

The army shows few signs of philosophic disaffection. Military leaders seem to be at least as fundamentalist as the party leaders. The aspect of Marxism-Leninism which might trouble the military is its equalitarianism, whereby the ordinary workers are the salt of the earth. The hierarchic and class separation in the Soviet army is extreme, with differences of pay, accommodations, and social position about as marked as in any army in the world. A sailor is paid five rubles per month, a lieutenant five hundred, an admiral two thousand. The generals are a class apart. Each group has its special perquisites, down to the quality of tobacco furnished. The army reconciles real differences of privileges with the demands of ideology in much the same way the party does, by mixing pretensions of paternalism and symbolic camaraderie with the realities of status.

Marxism-Leninism provides the men of arms with a permanent enemy and a supreme mission of world order. The soldierly spirit is unfriendly to mercantile capitalism even without the benefit of Marxism; and so far as the army has a political purpose, it is identical with that of the party, the preservation of the united rulership of the Soviet domain, the multinational Soviet "family of nations" plus the satellites. Party and army lean on each other in the repression of dissident movements and in the possible further spread of Soviet authority. It is hard to guess how far the torrent of military indoctrination is really designed to raise defensive capacities and how far it serves political aims; paramilitary training makes a population not only better prepared to fight but easier to rule.

The politicized military establishment is so intermeshed with the armylike party that the two are not really separate organizations. Rather, the army is the adjunct of the party for custody of physical force and its possible use in the same way that the Komsomol is the party's affiliate for mobilizing and directing the youth and the trade-union system is the affiliate of the party for organization of workers. If military men come to play a larger role in Soviet political life, it seems probable that this will be within, not against, the Soviet system. If a general were in command of the Soviet government, he would be constrained to invent something like the party if it were not at hand to help him manage the realm.

Leninism has been successful not in the revolutionizing of developed countries but in the more or less military mobilization of less developed lands. Leninist patterns not only won against odds the civil war and the Great Patriotic War in the Soviet Union but have reaped spectacular victories against materially superior forces in Yugoslavia, China, and Vietnam. Communism has risen to its full potential, harnessed with militant nationalism.

PART THREE

HOW
THE SOVIET SYSTEM
WORKS

CHAPTER 10

The Keeping of Order

According to Marxist theory and the aspirations of the revolution, crime should disappear in the socialist harmony. Lenin expected this to happen and only belatedly took steps to provide his state with laws and courts. Yet after five decades, crime, supposedly a typical byproduct of capitalism, remains a major Communist problem. There is very little reporting of it, except of incidents that make moral points. But the Soviet press, even while claiming victories over crime, frequently returns to the attack; and new measures are always found necessary.

A frequent explanation is that crime is ascribable to hostile actions of the imperialists, to their insidious poisoning of minds, and to their agents; it is considered transitory, the product of "bourgeois" selfishness and individualism, or a survival of prerevolutionary ways and mentality.

In more realistic discussions, many other causes are admitted, including mismanagement of the economy which causes speculation in deficit goods, bad living conditions, improper organization of security forces, and above all alcoholism. Whatever the cause, the individual is entirely responsible. Moreover, ordinary civil crime, in the Soviet system, merges into political crime. Just as it is an expression of loyalty and Communist discipline to work well, it is politically bad to cheat or steal public, or state, property or to loaf on the job. On the other hand, political oppositionists, like the writers Daniel and Siniavsky, are usually treated as speculators and unprincipled coveters of Western material rewards.

ARBITRARY FORCE

The Soviet state has always been inclined to deal with political opposition in a political, more or less arbitrary, fashion, without the restraints of a regular court procedure. Lenin put a political police, the Cheka, to work soon after the revolution while the Soviet court system was still embryonic. Illegal executions began in February, 1918; and Lenin frequently berated his heavy-handed lieutenants for softness. After the wounding of Lenin in August, 1918, thousands of persons with no connection with the deed were executed. Terrorism became a regular weapon of the Bolsheviks (and of their opponents) in the civil war.

Throughout the 1920's, terrorism was relatively mild, and political prisoners were usually treated leniently, somewhat in line with tsarist custom. Under Stalin, however, terrorism became a prime principle of government; the police apparatus, successively named GPU, OGPU, NKVD, or MVD, became one of the major powers at Stalin's right hand, a political force with some autonomy.

The political importance of the police was diminished with the execution of Beria. Thereafter, the security police, now called KGB (Committee of State Security), became less conspicuous. Khrushchev, realizing the counterproductive effects of terror in the modern economy, may have desired to end arbitrary procedures altogether. He claimed to have no political prisoners in the Soviet Union, and there was begun an overhaul of the codes for the sake of "socialist legality."

Khrushchev's successors have reverted to semi-Stalinist methods. Much has been done to glorify the KGB, whose agents are given credit for the safety of the fatherland. About half a million strong, the KGB has recovered some political importance, but is covered by secrecy. It is regarded as a conservative, anti-Western force.

The Brezhnev government has thus far shown no inclination to revert to terrorism even on the reduced scale of Stalin's last years, probably because of fear that it would get out of control. However, it carries on quiet repression. Many citizens are kept under surveillance and intimidated. Some are imprisoned or deprived of residence permits. Others are threatened with loss of jobs, or fired; if discharged, they may become subject to deportation. A student who refuses to participate in elections may be expelled from school; one who passes out pamphlets may be sent to labor camp. There are several political mental hospitals, as the Soviet state has made common the practice rarely indulged by the tsarist regime of designating insane those vocal in disagreement and subjecting them to treatment by KGB men in white blouses.

Ordinary Russians learn of such actions only by gossip, however, and repressive measures lose much of their effectiveness because they are unpublicized. For this reason and because critical attitudes have become respectable, some Russians speak with considerable indifference to possible consequences.

FORMAL JUSTICE

For ordinary law enforcement, reliance is placed on the civil police ("militia"). The militia, like the armed forces, have political officers and operate under close party supervision. Unlike the armed forces, they do not appear in the published budget, and their numbers are a matter of conjecture.

The police turn offenders over to a court system formally resembling that of Western European countries, particularly that of Germany. The basic "people's court" for civil and criminal cases has a judge, usually a woman, "elected" by the people, and two laymen called "assessors" drawn from a panel made up by the party and accepted by workers' meetings. Above them are regional courts, republic supreme courts, and a USSR Supreme Court, nominally elected by corresponding soviets. In 1967 the Supreme Court had among its members two prominent KGB men. The judges have five-year terms, and judgeship is a profession. Judges can be recalled, however, and have no security. Higher courts, without lay assessors, hear appeals, which can be presented by either defense or prosecution.

Judges are supposed to act on the evidence of the case, but Soviet political theory rejects separation of powers, and Soviet sources candidly proclaim the party's guidance of the courts and the prosecutors, as of other institutions. Judges are understood to be party members. Since Stalin, however, much has been said of "socialist legality," and the state has increasingly tried to follow definite procedures; a regime interested in fixity has to subscribe to some rule of law. Apparently concrete evidence is ordinarily required for conviction, even of political defendants.

The conduct of trials differs from Western custom both in procedure and spirit. The decision as to guilt or innocence is usually made in a pretrial investigation, in which interrogation is unlimited and the accused has no counsel. The function of the court is principally to fix the degree of guilt and the appropriate punishment. Court procedure is decidedly informal. The judge largely conducts the trial, does most questioning of witnesses, and decides the sentence. The two lay assessors, who take the place of the jury of tsarist times, play a largely ornamental role. One of their functions is to explain decisions to the people and generally to support the law; they are another means of linking official organs with the masses. A prosecutor, called "procurator," and a defense lawyer are usually present, although these may be dispensed with in minor cases.

The defense plea is usually mitigating circumstances or good character, and much of the trial is likely to revolve around the record of the accused as a worker and Soviet citizen, a fact which should serve as an incentive for proper conduct of all citizens. The trial is not only for the benefit of the accused but for the edification of the public (unless it should have political significance and hence probably be closed). "Public accusers," or representatives of various "social organizations," may be brought in on either side, but usually appear for the prosecution. Trials may be held at factories to make them accessible to large audiences. The social nature of the crime is made clear to both defendant and spectators; it is much worse to steal state than private property.

The procuracy is a distinct and important organ of the Soviet government. It acts not only as prosecutor but as general guardian of legality. Highly centralized and independent of local powers, the procurator's office is supposed to be always on the watch for violations of law. It decides whether or not to prosecute, unless this decision is taken by a party organization which may hold a pretrial of the case and decide whether the accused is to be let off, reprimanded, or turned over to the state arm. The procurator is supposed to be at once a party to the case and an impartial agent of justice who may put in a word for the accused. He has a uniform not unlike that of a naval officer. The defense attorney is relatively humble, low in status, pay, and prestige. Lawyers receive a salary, and their career depends on pleasing not litigants but the authorities.

If the convict is well regarded, he may be given a suspended sentence and remanded to the custody of a collective, for example his factory, for reeducation. Otherwise, there may be a severe penalty for minor infractions: stealing a fur hat may bring two weeks' to five years' hard labor. The maximum term is fifteen years, with parole possible after ten. The only higher sentence is death. Capital punishment has had a checkered history in Russia and the Soviet Union, and the legal existence of the penalty has had little relation to the number of persons put to death by the state. In 1958 and 1961, as most of the world was moving in the opposite direction and Khrushchev's Russia was entering its most liberal phase, capital punishment was broadened for a number of grave crimes of violence and then for large-scale economic crimes, currency speculation, embezzlement, stealing of state property, etc.; there were frequent announcements of its application—mostly to Jews. There were no announced death sentences for crimes against property from the early 1960's until the summer of 1970.

In the work camp, the convict is to be at once made useful and spiritually redeemed by physical labor. He may also be required to attend "political training" sessions. There are several types of camps of varying degrees of severity. Under the ordinary regimen, five visits and three parcels per year are permitted. The prison population is a matter of speculation. The man who has served his time is often not free to go home, as he may be denied a residence permit or assigned to another area.

LAW

Law, like lawyers, has little prestige; it is something theoretically to be done away with in the Communist future. At first, the young Soviet state wanted to get rid of law immediately. Tsarist courts were abolished, and the old codes were to be applied only in terms of "revolutionary legal conscience." Soviet law was hardly more than the will of the party. With the end of the civil war and the retreat of the NEP, codes were adopted, blending Bolshevik, tsarist, and Western legal ideas, to regularize relations within a stable society. Up to the end of the 1920's Soviet theorists still looked to the imminent demise of state and law; but Stalin maintained that the state had to be strengthened in its repressive functions as the class struggle sharpened with the march of socialism to victory.

After Stalin, something was done to improve the legal system. The law of analogy, an elastic clause under which an act could be condemned as "analogous" to a prohibited act, was dropped. There were to be no more secret criminal laws, confession was no longer to be held sufficient proof of guilt, and the accused was given some guarantees. This movement toward better order in the legal system was climaxed by a new code in 1958. Soon afterwards, however, there was instituted a countertrend toward more "popular," or party-guided justice, with irregular "comrade courts" and mass meetings given power to exile "parasites." The post-Khrushchev leadership gave some promise of furthering "socialist legality" and turned idlers over to regular authorities, but it changed little in the legal structure. New codes were issued in several areas, but the most signal change was recentralization, as the republics lost the slight latitude they had acquired under Khrushchev. Emphasis has now turned from the "withering away" of the law to its "supreme flowering under socialism." There seems to be growing reliance on criminal penalties to secure economic or social aims. For example, in view of increasing traffic accidents, it was decreed in October, 1970, that drivers in fatal accidents might receive up to fifteen years imprisonment; pedestrians who caused accidents were made subject to five years.

Soviet law is exalted as qualitatively distinct and much higher than any hitherto known. For the most part, however, its provisions parallel those of other states, with some special prohibitions. It is a crime to give religious instruction, or to buy and sell for a profit, or to hire help to make something for sale, or even to make something alone for sale without specific license. The duties of the citizen are extensive. For example, it is a criminal offense to fail to control weeds in cultivated areas. A person without a regular job may be assigned work or, if he refuses, to forced labor. Soviet law also has peculiar fields such as housing rights, which acquire special importance because of the housing shortage and because occupying an apartment is almost tantamount to owning property. There are some differences of approach; for example, the planning of a crime is held equivalent to its commission.

Soviet law is also marked by applicability to political offenses, since articles in the published code cover any conceivable undesirable behavior. The prohibition of espionage can be applied to almost any information about the Soviet economy, technology, or culture, as well as to defense. The efforts of some Westerners to distribute leaflets in Moscow (February, 1970) was charged as "malicious hooliganism," maximum sentence five years, without reference to the content of the leaflets. The constitutional guarantees of freedom of speech, etc., must be exercised "in conformity with the interests of the workers and in order to strengthen the socialist state." Laws against anti-Soviet propaganda apply to religious and nationalistic agitation; the Crimean Tatars who petitioned for return to their homeland were convicted of this crime in August, 1968. Those who demonstrated against the occupation of Czechoslovakia were punished for "interference with traffic."

No matter what the law says, what counts is its application. On some occasions, strict rules may be diffidently applied or allowed to lapse. For example, Stalin's decrees on labor discipline were a dead letter for years before they were formally repealed. On the other hand, systematic practice may be counter to the letter of the law. Thus, the prohibition of emigration is an essential of the Soviet system. It is very difficult for ordinary Soviet citizens to get permission to depart the homeland; and to attempt it illegally is a capital crime. Even to apply for an exit visa is very bold. Yet according to the law travel is completely free.

JUSTICE BY THE PEOPLE

Having renounced Stalinist terror, Khrushchev developed or revived several agencies of control, the volunteer police ("druzhiny"), the informal petty "comrade" courts, and a variety of volunteer control groups. The ostensible purpose of these organizations was to prepare for the transition to the goal of pure communism, and they were supposed to represent a transfer of coercive authority from the official state to "social" organizations. The "popular" agencies, however, did not replace official organs but supplemented them.

The druzhiny are youths, numbering six to seven million, led by Komsomol activists, who give an evening now and then to patrolling the streets, wearing red armbands, on the lookout for antisocial behavior. Functioning directly under party organizations, they have the authority to detain persons and to bring them to the militia or other authority. For their activity they earn honors and presumably political credits. Less formally, Komsomol groups also often act as vigilantes, organizing "raids" on factories or farms or, more commonly, calling deviationist young people to order and censoring clothing, music, or dances.

The comrade courts are something between courts of justice and indignation meetings, summoned by the party to castigate minor evildoers. There may be three hundred thousand in the Soviet Union. They have a chairman and secretary but no prosecutor or defense attorney or rules of procedure. They deal mostly with disorderly conduct or petty quarrels, but also handle antisocial behavior with political significance.

Their purpose is primarily education, to show up the wayward before the assembled citizens and to induce them to repent and confess. They can, however, place a reprimand on one's record, impose small fines, and suggest stronger measures for others to carry out, such as demotion in employment, eviction from housing, or up to fifteen days physical labor at the workplace. This verdict can be appealed to the local soviet executive committee, which may return the case for retrial. There are also other semiofficial courts of "parental honor," "workers' honor," and the like. In minor infractions, the militia may turn the culprit over to his employer for chastisement.

There are various other agencies whereby social pressure is applied. Apartment committees assist political education, prevent violations of apartment rules, protect buildings, keep young folks from going astray, save marriages from breaking up, and help the police. Street committees sponsor lectures and other political entertainment, help schools, and fight petty crime. Juvenile affairs commissions, composed of soviet deputies, teachers, militia, and others, have extensive duties in connection with the guidance of juveniles and rights of punishment; they are even authorized to take children from their parents.

PEOPLE'S CONTROL

The most important agency of social control is the People's Control Committee, the head of which is a Politburo member. This forms an organization parallel with the party and soviet hierarchy—almost another arm of the political system. Leaders of local control committees direct control "groups" and "posts," of which there are about a million, manned by seven million volunteer inspectors and controllers. The controllers investigate, denounce the guilty, or publicize their findings; they may levy fines and suspend officials from their positions pending further inquiry. They look into all manner of inefficiency and malfeasance; pilferage of state property is their particular concern. They also act virtually as extensions of the party, studying the political and moral qualities of workers, helping to educate and organize the cadres, perhaps recommending candidates for responsible positions.

Party guidance is very close. Leaders of control groups are party members, while presidents of party control committees are generally party secretaries or committee members. The party also undertakes the political education of people's controllers, who are likely to be candidates for political advancement. The people's control apparatus is, in short, part of the Soviet system, another transmission belt through which the party makes its will effective. Its true importance remains to be seen, but the volunteer enforcers of law and morality could be the answer to an autocrat's prayer. They cost little, occupy many idealistic people and give them a sense of participation in public affairs, and keep everyone in society under some kind of surveillance; yet they represent no political force.

CHAPTER 11

Managing the Economy

INDUSTRY

The basic Soviet claim of superiority is that the means of production belong to the people. With no private ownership of factories, railroads, farms, and all other property which is used to create wealth, there should be no exploitation. The vices of the selfish bourgeois-capitalist order should be cast away. Production should soar as capitalist anarchy is replaced by rational socialist order. And peace and happiness should reign as class conflict disappears in the era of abundance and equality.

Marxists always took it for granted that private ownership, at least of large industrial plants, was to be ended by socialism; but it was not clear how the economy was then to be administered. Marx wrote much of "workers' associations." In 1917-18 there was much irregular workers' control in Russia, but this led to chaos and the state inevitably took over management as rapidly as it was able. In the civil war, nearly all industrial production was by command: goods were transferred without payment. To remedy the economic disaster that resulted from overcontrol and the civil war, Lenin made a major retreat in his New Economic Policy of 1921. But the Bolsheviks never surrendered the idea of central direction, and Stalin's First Five-Year Plan brought

158

more and more strict and detailed controls of all aspects of the economy. Centralized management resulted in considerable success in heavy industry, although at the cost of consumer goods production. But by the time of Stalin's death, controls were not adequate to manage the growing complexity of the economy and had to be modified to permit continued expansion. Many small steps were taken to give industrial managers a little more discretion in the use of resources; some materials were released from allocation, plants were permitted to sell surplus equipment, etc. But more was needed, and in 1957 Khrushchev put through extensive decentralization. Nearly all the economic ministries in Moscow, except those related to defense, were dissolved, although central planning was retained. The enterprises were transferred to a hundred-odd local economic councils. The decentralization was designed to bring the bureaucrats closer to the industries they supervised and to reduce transportation costs. However, it led to some localism and within a few years regional units were being created over the councils and many of these were amalgamated. At the same time, industrial growth failed to respond but continued to decline while the control apparatus continued to swell.

Economic reform was hence high on the agenda of the new government. Kosygin in 1965 outlined extensive changes pointing both to decentralization and recentralization: managers of industrial enterprises were to be given more latitude and encouraged to strive for a profit instead of merely fulfilling output figures, but the central economic ministries were to be restored. Of these two sides of the reform, the first was the more publicized, but recentralization proved more operative as the liberalizing reforms were watered-down in practice. However, there was no more grand campaigning, as there was when Stalin had given steel all-out priority, and Khrushchev had turned to the chemical industry as a cure-all. Targets were scaled down, and the plans were made less exciting and more realistic.

The main ideas of planning have changed little since the First Five-Year Plan. The conventional period has been five years; longer projections, for ten or twenty years, seem to have had little meaning. The five-year plan is described as legally compulsory, but is mostly a political goal. Year-to-year plans are more operative; these are projections based on experience and the performance of the previous year.

The principal planning agency, Gosplan, assisted by a number of commissions, translates party directives into figures, primarily of goods to be produced but also covering many other performance indices such as labor productivity, cost reduction, return on investment, material consumption, and innovation. Gosplan then allots corresponding demands to the republics and provinces. These divide obligations among smaller territorial divisions, and so on down to individual factories, shops within factories, brigades, and even individual workers. There is always a contest between higher-ups, who want their inferiors to promise to produce as much as possible with the least possible input of resources, and the subordinates, who wish to get as much labor, capital, and materials as possible for the smallest assignments they can wangle.

Plan fulfillment is the prime criterion of success for producers (and to a large extent for transportation agencies, distributors, et al.), determining whether they get bonuses or penalties. Within the limitation of planned goals, multiple controls, and the restriction that materials must be bought from prescribed suppliers and sales made to prescribed users, the manager buys and sells and employs the resources at his disposition as he decides best. He operates on a budget and tries to make a profit, part of which he, like an American corporate executive, can retain for various uses, and part of which, as in the United States, goes into the state treasury.[1] He cannot make major investment decisions, as capital is allocated by the state. He cannot fix prices, which are set by official agencies, and which partly reflect costs, partly priorities.

If the planning system were able effectively to direct energies and materials, the Soviet Union would have long since outstripped the most productive of the disorderly capitalist countries. In practice, the planned Soviet economy has been able to direct a large share of the national income into investment, and has achieved a high rate of growth over a long time by concentration on essentials. But it suffers many ills that offset its advantages.

A basic difficulty of planning is that there is no good way to measure output, and whatever criterion is adopted leads to distortions. It is impossible to have quotas for each product except in the simplest industries, so the planners have usually chosen a gross aggregate measure, like weight, numbers, etc. But if cloth is counted by weight, it is made as heavy as possible; if by area, thin; if by length, narrow; if by price, costly. Machines added up by weight become steel monsters. To fulfill plans, railroads send freight a roundabout route. Sometimes for simplicity the plan has been in terms of materials consumed, an invitation to maximize waste.

The planners can use monetary levers, but there is no good way to set prices. Failure to take into account capital has meant waste, and there is little stimulus to efficiency and cost reduction. Labor and materials are hoarded; construction projects drag out interminably. Local initiative is stifled as managers await orders from overburdened central authorities. Factories complain that they are buried in forms and drowned in often contradictory directives. Multiple and overlapping controls tie up producers without preventing cheating. Since quotas and allotments are so important in terms of bonuses, there is every incentive to fool those higher up both as to needs and capacities. Inflation in production figures is inevitable, scrap is counted as output, and managers pad costs and labor needs. The ministry may not desire to uncover the fakery, because this would detract from its own results. It is probably impossible for a manager to fill his plans, in view of deficiencies of supply, without engaging in illegal operations. Fixers and expeditors who seek ways around red tape play a major role in the Soviet economy. Half of all travel in the Soviet Union is said to be connected with deficiencies of the supply system.[2] More or less officially tolerated, black or gray market private enterprise looms large and has probably been growing in recent years. Illegal buying and selling in controlled markets mean easy enrichment; for example, dealers who find a supply of beans can make a profit of 1000%.[3] It seems to be quite normal for collective farms to buy lumber from unofficial dealers and no one minds unless the dealer turns out to be a cheat. Local industries are set up to manufacture such things as curlers and pens from materials of unknown, that is, illegal provenance. Small construction jobs are apparently quite often done by private operators. Some free enterprise seems to be essential to make planning workable.

The result is not that the system cannot produce but that production is costly and poorly adapted to needs of the market. The system functions well in those areas which receive closest attention from central authorities and enjoy high prestige. There is no indication that Soviet armaments are inferior to the best; and related branches like aircraft production and watches have also done well. Planning is also relatively successful in industries which have simple, large-scale, and unchanging products such as coal and steel. But progress means more fabrication, more specialized expertise, an ever increasing number of products, and interrelations in the economy growing approximately as the square of the number of products. It has become ever harder to decide what should be produced and to devise ways of inducing people to produce what is most needed at the minimum cost.

For the most part, the remedies are much like those of a decade or a generation ago. From time to time, there are calls for improved labor discipline and campaigns for cracking down on loafers and drifters. In 1970-71 many industrial plants were amalgamated into larger combines to reduce overlap and supposedly permit more efficient planning. Prices have been restudied and juggled to encourage innovation. The role of the party in guidance of the economy has been raised; perhaps more than ever before the party is to concern itself with nuts and bolts. Party discipline and spirit should compensate for inadequacies of the planning mechanism. There has also been a great deal of emphasis on moral incentives to better efforts, manifold honors for the best workers and shame for the slackers.

Basic reform, however, is difficult. The Russians have invented no way of making huge bureaucracies more flexible and rational than in other lands. The fact that all productive goods are owned by the state makes political management seem natural; transfers of materials are not truly sales, as ownership does not change. Prices are more or less arbitrary and so not an adequate basis for economic decisions. Planners, having political power, think in terms of solving problems by command or administrative action. They prefer having a commission control quality or plan assortment rather than leaving it to consumer preference. The idea of individual or group gain is in bad repute in the collectivist society, and it is difficult to divorce the idea of gain from productivity and efficiency. Probably the Soviet Union is condemned to a relatively low level of efficiency, in terms of output in relation to input, until it produces the new Soviet Man or devises a much looser economic structure.

TRADE-UNIONS

The trade-unions are important auxiliaries of the party in the stimulation of production and promotion of labor discipline. Nearly all workers, except the temporarily employed, are members; and unions include not only bench workers but managers, who may be quite influential within the workers' organization.

The trade-unions are controlled from top down. Candidates for leading positions are recommended from above; and union officials, like party secretaries, are subject to confirmation. They are also controlled by the party at each level. Elections are much like those in the party. Ordinary members may rarely express disapproval of a candidate, but there is no question of anyone unacceptable to the party being elected. As Soviet authors frankly put it, if the unions themselves proposed candidates, this would be harmful to the dictatorship of the proletariat.[4] The duty of the trade-union to follow the party is written into the statutes, and they, like the soviets, are practically an extension of the party. When the Central Council of Trade Unions met in July, 1969, the only item on the agenda was, "Results of the International Meeting of Communist and Workers' Parties." Any independence of unions is inadmissible because it would bring out latent conflicts of material interests between workers and the state which runs the factories.

As agents of the state, trade-unions handle social security benefits (except pensions), health services, and sanatoria; they sponsor and largely finance vacations for deserving workers. They patronize organized sports, which are as politicized in the Soviet Union as they are commercialized in the West. They have some voice in housing assignment, the payment of overtime, job classification, and the utilization of collective bonuses. Unions also should protect the worker in various ways; they must be consulted regarding disciplinary actions, especially dismissal—a serious blot on the record of the Soviet worker. It is important for a worker to stand well with his union.

Unions sign collective contracts with management. Because wages are fixed by the government, they deal mostly with the joint efforts of workers and management to fulfill the plan, the most important function of the unions. This they do not only by propaganda and moral pressure but by their ability to assist the workers and to reward the zealous. It is also a function of the unions to prevent strikes and work stoppages. Although wages are beyond the powers of management, there have been occasional reports of strikes from sundry exasperations. A strike means that union leaders (as well as party and management) have failed, and they can expect to be appropriately punished.

AGRICULTURE

The Soviet system is better adapted to industry than agriculture. The productivity of Soviet labor in industry is about half of the American, in agriculture only a quarter. Industrial output has grown many fold since 1928. Agricultural output was for a long time less than before the Bolsheviks took it over and to date has grown only moderately. The party calls again and again for improvement, measures are taken, but agriculture remains the weakest side of the Soviet economy. In 1970, the Central Committee and the Council of Ministers demanded better attention to the procurement of wild fruits and berries and wild honey.[5]

Marxism was not for peasants; they did not fit its theories and it had little to offer them. Industrialization, on the other hand, promised social transformation, a desired industrial proletariat, and an economy controllable by the party. Most of all, perhaps, industry meant military power. Agriculture bespoke consumption goods, always of secondary interest, and has shared the neglect of light industry. For similar reasons, agriculture has commonly been neglected in underdeveloped countries;

it does not appeal to leaders as the way out of backwardness to power and glory.

Collectivization made it possible for the state to expropriate the peasants' labor with minimal return: "The First Commandment is grain for the state."[6] To make collectivization bearable, peasant households have been permitted to use a plot of as much as an acre for themselves to raise potatoes or vegetables and keep a cow with calf (pastured to collective land), some pigs, chickens, or other small stock, according to the region. Produce of the garden plots (along with pay received in kind from the collective) may be sold on free markets, of which there are about eight thousand in the Soviet Union. The private plots were so much more productive than the collectivized fields that they were the major source of sustenance in Stalin's day; putting in the required number of labor-days for the collective was the price for being allowed a household plot. They still make a disproportionate contribution to the peasants' income and the Soviet diet.

Since 1930 the collective farms have been completely controlled by party and state. They are governed much as other Soviet organizations. Theoretically, the assembly of members is sovereign; it elects a chairman and other officers designated by the party. Membership is fixed, and a peasant can withdraw from the collective farm, (or "kolkhoz"), or even make a trip to the city, only by permission. His grown children become kolkhoz members automatically, unless they decline to return after military service or manage to be admitted to higher educational institutions. However, the collectives are legally an anomaly in the Soviet system, with their theoretically cooperative ownership of means of production. For ideological-political reasons, the Soviet ideal has always been the state farm ("sovkhoz"), which is an agricultural factory, as much a part of the apparatus as a steel mill, directly and unequivocally under ministerial orders. Consequently, the general thrust of Soviet policy since the Second World War has been toward the fuller incorporation of the kolkhozes into the Soviet system.

Through amalgamations, the collective farms have been made huge, impersonal organizations, the average now having some 2800 hectares of arable land, 6100 hectares in all, a thousand head of cattle, forty tractors, 420 households and 1400 souls. For equipment operators and other skilled personnel there is a trade-union, as though they were employees, not members. The peasants were formerly to be compensated by sharing out, through a complex and unequal scheme, whatever was left after all obligations were met. Lately, an attempt has been made to pay collective farmers regularly to make them more like wage-earners, and thereby to increase their willingness to work on the collective fields and to reduce dependence on private plots. From 1965, there were also moves to provide them small pensions. Further to approximate kolkhoz to sovkhoz, there has been intermittent pressure on the peasant plot, supposedly one day to be abandoned. It seems likely that the difference between the two types will eventually be erased.

The giant state farms now come close to providing half of the Soviet food supply. Spread over tens of thousands of hectares and comprising dozens or scores of villages, more mechanized and more productive than the kolkhoz, they should approach the Communist planners' dreams. They have several specialized departments, of agronomy, animal husbandry, communal services, construction, and planning, each headed by supposed experts and staffed by specialized workers more like factory-bound proletarians than individualistic, tradition-bound and inaccessible peasants. The modern sovkhoz should, in the Marxist way, be growing toward an urban style of life, with large apartment buildings, cafeterias, nurseries, cinema, and the like. However, it is something of a white elephant, expensive and cumbersome. Both sovkhoz and kolkhoz, as Soviet economists are well aware, are badly in need of decentralization, much as industry needs more latitude for economic profit-and-loss management.

The debate has gone on in agriculture even longer than in industry in the form of efforts to enlarge or restrict the "link" as a unit of production and accounting. There have been moves to let "links" — groups of some six to twelve peasants—take charge of a fixed parcel of land with livestock and as much equipment as feasible and cultivate it as well as they could for their own material benefit. The farmers would pay a "rent" in the form of sales of fixed quantities of produce at fixed prices; whatever else they could raise they could merchandise freely. This has been tried out with reportedly excellent results, but it is feared that such a change might lead to the breakup of the collectives and a retreat from economic planning, to weakening of the party's position in the countryside, and to dissolution of much of the administrative apparatus.

CONTROLS AND DIFFICULTIES

Lines of authority over agriculture go through the All-Union and republic ministries of agriculture, the soviets, and the party. Primary responsibility for management of agriculture lies with the county ("raion") administration, which looks to deliveries; virtually all collective farm programs are determined by the assignments given to them. Chairmen are regularly brought in from the outside to check self-seeking tendencies on the part of the kolkhoz. Socially and politically superior to the ordinary members, they are professionals, probably trained in special schools, whose advancement depends on satisfying the party hierarchy. The chairman is a more powerful boss than an industrial manager since the collective farmers are more scattered than factory workers and have less recourse to agencies which might protect their rights. He can dispose freely of kolkhoz funds and property as long as he fulfills his obligations to the state. He assigns jobs and issues binding orders to all under him, who are not free to leave the estate. He may even require his subjects to give blood.[7]

He has little autonomy, however. It is more difficult to plan agriculture from a distance than industry, as farms have their particular problems in endlessly varied local conditions, and the weather perennially presents uncertainties. Yet distant authorities give all manner of overriding instructions regarding what is to be planted and how. Each administrative layer is under pressure from above to extract as much as possible from those below, and party and state agencies interfere constantly, with or without strict legal authority, to overcome what they see as backwardness or selfishness on the part of producers. If a farm produces a large amount of milk or grain, its quota is likely to be raised. If farmers make money by producing high quality pickles, they are scolded and warned that wealth will not bring them happiness.[8] A good harvest may be actually harmful as it encourages the secretaries and directors to suppose that they can interfere with impunity and squeeze the household plots, while a bad harvest inspires respect for realities. When it is announced that farms can sell their produce freely or at higher prices, over fixed quotas, this is negated by calls for voluntary overfulfillment, for joyous contributions to socialist competition, or for generous assistance to less fortunate kolkhozes.

Planning encounters many troubles similar to those in industry. The demand for paperwork is insatiable. A sovkhoz may have fifteen or sixteen thousand indicators in its long-range plan, and may be expected to supply fifty to sixty thousand indices throughout the year.[9] The measurement of performance is difficult. When the chicken-tenders were paid by the weight of chickens raised, they produced hens too fat for laying; it proved necessary to go to such criteria as the amount of vitamin A in their livers and the size of the oviduct.[10] Judicial sanctions are used to supplement economic incentives; loss of cotton in harvesting is punishable by a year's imprisonment, two years if the fiber is taken for home use.[11] The complex pricing system suffers multiple rigidities and irrationalities discouraging initiative and improvement; for example, prices fixed through the year discourage off-season production and storage of perishables.

Under these conditions, Soviet agriculture has suffered lethargy and inefficiency. Conditions of labor are still poor; a milkmaid may go to work at 3 or 4 AM, and not return home until late in the evening.[12] In 1971, the Soviet Union was still mobilizing cadres to fight the "grain battle." Every fall, quantities of foodstuffs are lost because of lack of storage and transportation facilities. A large part of agricultural machinery is regularly reported idle and in need of spare parts or repairs. Misuse of collective assets seems to be rife. The relative productivity of the household plots gives some measure of the depth of the trouble. Producing a third of agricultural output on 1% of cultivated land, in 1970 they accounted for 60% of potatoes, 45% of vegetables, 40% of meat and milk, and 60% of eggs, figures which had declined only slightly over the previous decade. Privately owned Soviet pigs performed about as well as the American average; socialized pigs put on less than half as much weight.[13] The productivity of labor seems to be as high on the diminutive plots as on the immense collective fields with all their machines and large-scale facilities.[14]

Despite this poor record, however, the Russian village is gradually moving into the twentieth century. The Stalinist neglect is no more; agriculture is no longer called upon to finance industrialization but receives growing investment funds—allotments for 1971-75 are set at 77.6 billion rubles, 70% over the previous five-year period. Peasant incomes have doubled and tripled in the post-Stalin years. Electric lines are creeping across the countryside, and television sets are no longer a rarity. The peasant is still a second-class citizen, but the Bolsheviks have made peace with him.

RESULTS AND PROSPECTS

The Soviet is somewhat like a war economy, not only because of shortages, stresses, and priorities, but in its campaigning, relative neglect of the consumer, and use of noneconomic methods and moral incentives. For some purposes, it is effective, perhaps more so than any other method imaginable. It is able to shift resources, to make major decisions and to concentrate on objectives which the planners or the party deem crucial. It should be well equipped to plan urban development, at least in broad outlines. It produces magnificent displays, from May Day celebrations to spectacular theatricals. Some basic services, like medicine and education, are well organized and more broadly available than in most countries. Public transportation is generally efficient and inexpensive. Military wares are outstanding both in quality and quantity.

The level of Soviet technology and productivity varies somewhat according to relation to military and national political purposes. The space program, run by the military, was ahead of the American as long as it could ride on military rocketry and fell behind only when the United States developed rockets larger than militarily useful. Various items, such as helicopters and cameras, benefit from military priority. The Soviet fishing fleet is modern and efficient, although crews are about double those on comparable Japanese or Norwegian trawlers. If it seems easier to mechanize fishing than egg production, this is attributable to the naval and political utility of the fishing fleet. The Russians have much to boast of, likewise, in areas subsidiary to military production. Steel technology has been up to international standards, and production indicators for Soviet furnaces are quite high.

Agriculture and consumer goods industry have by contrast been deficient because of lower priority, lower morale, and greater difficulty of central planning in these areas. Trade and distribution have suffered at least as much. Commerce seems to need freedom even more than industry; but distribution is a state monopoly (except for the kolkhoz markets) run on plans for turnover and fixed margins, with few incentives for initiative and many controls. Scorned as nonproductive, retail trade is one of the least desirable of professions.

By virtue of concentration on heavy industry and mobilization of resources, the Soviet Union has shown historically rapid growth. Industrial production increased yearly 12-14% in the decade after 1928 and at a similar rate in the decade after the Second World War. Soviet industrial production was about 13% of that of the United States in 1913, but it has been about two-thirds of that of the United States since 1963. In the late 1920's, Soviet steel production was less than one-fifth of the American, but it currently has been about equal. A number of countries, however, from Japan to Spain, have shown more rapid expansion in the last decade than the Soviet Union, some by a wide margin. In various aspects the Soviet economy is decidedly backward. For a larger population, the volume of mail and the number of telephones are less than one-tenth of the American figures. And the rise of the Soviet standard of living has not been comparable to industrial growth. Consumption per head is ordinarily estimated to be about half of that of leading Western European countries and a quarter of that of the United States, although comparisons are subjective and uncertain.

The average wage was supposed to reach 122 rubles (officially $146) monthly in 1971, with prices irregularly higher than in the United States. But quality, assortment, and availability are as important as wages and prices. Rents are low, in the range of five to ten dollars per month for small apartments. But housing is very short, with most urban families doubled up; housing per capita in the cities is still much under the prerevolutionary level. Tenants may have to make repairs or replace defective fixtures shortly after moving in. A large proportion of apartments lack running water. Many prerevolutionary buildings in Moscow and Leningrad are in excellent condition, while Soviet buildings frequently become shabby in a few years. To this day, tourists in the principal cities are likely to be lodged in tsarist-built hotels.

Another large area of continuing Soviet backwardness is the automotive industry. Production of passenger cars has been about a twentieth of the American, two-thirds of them destined for official use. By 1975, this may rise to a tenth, but the country is totally unprepared for the automotive age in roads, repair facilities, and service stations, of which Moscow recently had one per million population.

Many ordinary commodities are likely to be scarce. Sundry items, nylon stockings, irons, or hairpins, may be unobtainable or may glut the market when planners overreact to demand. During much of 1969, matches were a black market commodity. Transistor radios came to the Soviet Union with a lag of a decade; and the planners did not interest themselves in such trivia as cellophane tape, pencil sharpeners, can openers, and ballpoint pens. Principal Soviet cities in the latter 1960's opened shops wherein all manner of otherwise unobtainable and good quality merchandise could be purchased only with foreign currency. One commodity almost always to be bought for rubles at moderate prices is vodka.

The average Russian spends several hundred hours yearly waiting in front of shops or in line. For many goods, there is rationing by queue, as a shipment of stylish sweaters or pretty dishes is likely to be sold out in hours. Productivity of labor is reduced by workers' taking time off to get things repaired, do their shopping, or deal with official red tape. One learns of what is to be had only by word of mouth or by making the rounds of stores; commercial advertising is generally limited to such injunctions as "Drink coffee" or "Scallops are good eating."

Compared to the average person in most of the world, the Soviet consumer is well-off. Many appliances, for example television sets, refrigerators, and washing machines, are gradually becoming available to the mass of the population. It is in terms of results compared with ostensible efforts that the Soviet economy falls short; exhortation, prodding, indoctrination, organization, and the long-term dedication to building up the economy through the sacrifice of today to a promised tomorrow, have all worked no miracles. Apparently the great political effort to raise productivity is largely offset by a corresponding amount of politically induced waste.

Roughly from 1950 to 1960, output of steel, electricity, and other basic materials increased steeply. By 1959, Soviet industry acquired new equipment in the amount of $18 billion while new American industrial equipment came only to $9 billion. It seemed likely that the Soviet Union might soon offer its people at least more or less the same range of goods as Western Europe. The Soviet government promised categorically in 1961 that "in the current decade the Soviet Union . . . will surpass the strongest and richest capitalist country, the United States of America, in production per capita." But the gap between the Soviet Union and the United States has been little narrowed in the time which the Soviet leaders gave themselves to end it, despite the fact that for a decade Soviet investments in the economy have probably exceeded American. Japan, with less than half the Soviet population, threatens to surpass Soviet industrial production and is already far ahead in the most modern branches, like electronics. The share of the Soviet bloc in world trade has remained virtually unchanged. It is widely agreed that the Soviet technological lag has increased in the past decade; in computers at the end of 1970 the Soviet Union ranked sixth in the world behind France. Soviet growth rates have ceased to be a real argument for the superiority of the Soviet way.

Many reasons have been suggested for this slowdown, but the real problem seems to be the overuse or abuse of power. In the Soviet system, a man can acquire goods and status more readily by skill in dealing with people than by contributing to the production of material things. Relaxation of price control or simple measures of decentralization are unacceptable to the party because they would represent some loss of control or an opportunity for local people to become wealthy. Competition between nationalized enterprises would promise radical improvement for the market; this also is politically excluded. With no expenditure, the Soviet leadership could rapidly ease shortages by permitting small scale private enterprise in services, trade, and manufacturing. But this would permit large numbers of persons to earn their livelihood outside the official economy and thus to enjoy economic and potentially political independence. From the Soviet point of view, a person who earns money by individual endeavor is antisocial, that is, antistate. Overregulation nullifies initiative; people sit and wait for orders. It also means that a great part of the energies of the population is spent unproductively on control.

The maturing economy, however, presses against its bonds; the thesis that modernization entails liberalization of the political order is not without merit. The complexity of the economy defies the controllers, who cannot know nearly as much of what goes on as do the producers. It raises a large class of technicians who are less ideologically inclined than the party bosses. Rapid technological change makes it harder to sustain a fixed view of the world. It becomes more difficult to keep Soviet society essentially isolated from the heretical outside world. Scientific industrial development needs freedom to experiment and innovate, to generate and apply ideas. It threatens to breed the same kind of pluralism which enfeebled tsarist autocracy in its last decades.

FOOTNOTES

1. The state's share of industrial profits furnishes over a third of revenues. The second largest item is the turnover tax, which amounts to a sales tax at rates which are not publicized but which vary from about 20% to 300% or more on luxury goods. Income tax is low, with a maximum rate of 13% on salaries. A state lottery contributes to revenue. Inheritance tax was abolished in 1943.
2. *Izvestia*, January 21, 1971.
3. *Bakinskii rabochii,* October 31, 1970.

4. A. Aimbetov, M. Baimakonov, and M. Imashev, *Problemy sovershenstvovaniia organizatsii i deiatel'nosti mestnykh sovetov* (Izd. Nauka, Alma Ata, 1967), p. 84.

5. *Pravda*, April 7, 1970.

6. *ibid*, headline, September 2, 1971.

7. *Izvestia*, January 7, 1970; *ABSEES*, July, 1970, p. 84.

8. *Sovetskaia Rossiia*, October 30, 1970.

9. Morris Bornstein, "The Soviet Debate on Agricultural Price and Procurement Reforms," *Soviet Studies*, vol. 21, no. 1, July, 1969, p. 16.

10. *Sovetskaia Rossiia*, October 30, 1970.

11. *Pravda Vostoka*, November 5, 1970.

12. *Pravda*, September 16, 1970.

13. W. Klatt, *Soviet Agriculture: The Permanent Crisis*, ed. Roy D. Laird (Praeger, N.Y., 1965), p. 140.

14. Eric Strauss, *Soviet Agriculture in Perspective* (Praeger, New York, 1969), p. 189.

CHAPTER 12

Management of Minds

PERSUASION

Political culture in the West is produced by the press, schools, broadcasting, and cinema, along with popular traditions and inherited attitudes, all more or less independent of the government. In the Soviet Union all organized opinion-making (with the slight exception of churches) is closely directed by the party. Marxism claims that the ruling classes make a cultural superstructure to reinforce their position; nowhere do they do this so thoroughly and purposefully as in the Soviet Union. The monopoly of organization entails a monopoly of mass communication.

The lesser aspect of opinion control is officially unacknowledged censorship under the Ministry of Culture. Actual censorship comes only when material is put into print, and editors are supposed to be the primary watchdogs through their knowledge of what is expected. The more important means of control is to place in charge of newspapers, broadcasting stations, etc., trustworthy party men; to be a Soviet journalist is to be an especially reliable Communist.

Most of the press is directly under party management, while radio and television are run by state committees. With minor exceptions, all periodicals are published by party-controlled organizations, ranging from ministries to the Union of Writers. The most authoritative paper is *Pravda*, the party organ. On rare occasions papers have mildly criticized one another, and *Pravda* may criticize other papers, but no one criticizes *Pravda*. The press is a lever for the organization of the people, a coordinator of campaigns and means by which they learn the party line and concerns of the day. It is also a control organ. On the basis of letters received (major papers claim to receive a thousand or more letters per day) and information from reporters, who have full rights of access to lower-level offices, to question and examine almost anyone or anything, the press is an adjunct of more regular enforcement agencies. When even a local paper barks, party organizations jump, not to speak of nonparty ones.

Yet the quality of Soviet papers is not up to the importance attributed to them. Paper, printing, and pictures are mediocre to poor, and they ordinarily consist of only four pages. Many verbose statements seem intended for ideologists or party men only, and sometimes newspapers read like an official gazette. Reporting of the 1971 Party Congress consisted of speeches delivered, without commentary or summaries. There is little or no space for such things as crime (unless to point out a moral), merely personal news, and transportation or industrial accidents. Natural calamities ordinarily trouble only the non-Soviet world.

Every means of conveying information, from banners to speakers on the railroads, should likewise advance the "struggle for communism." Billboards give the slogans or caricature leading capitalist powers, and hardly a square is without its statue of Lenin. Radio Moscow gives the word to the world and the Soviet people; it takes precedence over local stations, which generally relay its programs in the same way that central papers stand above local organs. Television has become very important. Over six million sets were made in 1970; soon nearly all Soviet citizens should have access to television. The Russians also make much use of motion pictures. Not only long films, but documentaries, shorts, newsreels, and educational movies are used, somewhat as the American armed forces employ training films.

However, the party stresses face-to-face contact, which ranges from lectures and guided discussions to talks to the workers as they eat lunch; agitators are supposed to go around parks and kolkhoz markets engaging people in enlightening conversation. Workers or farmers should gather for "agitation" sessions, perhaps lightened by music or other amusement. The propagandists, said to number over two million, perhaps a half million of them professionals, have to be informative and interesting yet to stress correct ideology. Great efforts should be made to involve the people in their own indoctrination, to speak not so much to them as with them, to carry them along in the development of ideas. Leisure time should be edifying; best of all, perhaps, is volunteer labor, combining agitation and involvement with production. 119,200,000 persons are reported to have toiled on one Communist Saturday.[1]

A more singularly Soviet means of molding opinion is through party schools under the Propaganda Department of the Central Committee. These train at all levels of education and importance and in many forms both party and nonparty people, from high-ranking ideological specialists to part-time agitators to citizens brushing up their Marxism-Leninism. Everyone in a strictly political position, from the leader of a party group on up, is supposed regularly to participate in some form of political education. At the pinnacle is the Academy of Social Sciences to train topflight ideologists in a three-year course of instruction. Those of second rank may go to a Higher Party School in Moscow or in a republic capital or possibly study by correspondence. There are local political schools in considerable variety for the elite and the nonparty, including universities of Marxism-Leninism, Basic Marxism-Leninism schools, elementary party schools, party aktiv schools, study circles, theoretical seminars, schools of Communist labor, "People's Universities," and Houses of Political Enlightenment. The Komsomol has another, smaller network of political schools, in which most Komsomol youth are supposed to participate. More than a million Muscovites (about a quarter of the adult population) were recently reported studying Marxism-Leninism under ninety thousand instructors and lecturers, two-hundred thousand agitators, and fifty-two thousand "political informers."[2] It is very virtuous to participate; and in theory it might continue all one's life.

EDUCATION

The Soviet dedication to propaganda is inseparable from the dedication to education. The one should make politically schooled people; the other should train productive, morally and politically tempered citizens. Education is also an area of major success of the Soviet system which takes pride equally in having raised the country from relative backwardness to the world's second industrial power and in having turned a largely illiterate nation into one of the world's more educated. According to its statistics, the Soviet Union is the world's most advanced in technical training, with by far the world's largest pool of scientists and engineers. Perhaps more than anywhere else, in the Soviet Union education is the road to advancement; and nowhere else is it more expected that one prepare formally for his work. Not only mechanics and miners should have their diploma; textile workers and retail clerks should also be graduates of technical institutes.

The educational system is under centralized and multiple control. Since 1966, the Moscow Ministry of Education and the Ministry of Higher Education have had full control of curriculum and staffing. With slight deviations, all Soviet children of a given age should be studying the same lessons on the same day. The Ministry of Higher Education has to approve higher degrees and appointments to professorships. All university teachers are supposed to carry on ideological work. Local party committees and party organizations in schools supervise the teaching of history and social studies in the schools, consider staff nominations, and forward the political education of teachers.

The Soviet school has come full circle from the revolutionary years, when entrance requirements, examinations, and grades were abolished. Discipline is strict, and students are expected to acquire a large amount of information in both humanities and sciences. Scientific and technological courses comprise over half the curriculum of primary and secondary schools. Higher education is extremely specialized, designed not for enlightenment but for skills that prepare persons for particular slots in the national economy. Of more than six-hundred thousand yearly graduates of higher schools, nearly half are engineers or agronomists. Facilities are uneven, from the first-class universities to neglected rural schools, and schools suffer some of the same kind of troubles as the economy, from shortages of textbooks to difficulty of innovation. But Soviet education seems to be productive of technical competence.

However, "the Soviet school does not merely prepare educated people. From its halls there should come forth politically trained, ideally convinced builders of communism, patriots and internationalists."[3] "We want to educate our children to be toilers, persons for whom labor is the alpha and omega of life, its meaning and highest joy."[4] In kindergarten, children sing about Lenin and his love for them. They learn to sit immobile and respect the teacher and their elders, to admire heroes of war and labor, to love their "Socialist Fatherland," and to behave honorably as Lenin wished. Stress is laid upon collectivism and duty, belonging to the country and to the school group, and community property. The class is organized somewhat as a party group, with its committee and the teacher as secretary; the discipline and standing of the group are the responsibility of each and all. Competition is avoided; better students should help the weaker as all progress together. All share in the disciplining of deviants and learn thereby. There are honors of all kinds, the board or book of honor, badges, etc. Most of all, the child is to become accustomed to doing everything as part of an organized group engaged in planned activities. As a result, young Russians are said to be decidedly more mannerly and better disciplined than their American counterparts.

Ideological training begins in elementary school, as the child learns about the inevitable victory of communism, the leading role of the party, and the misery of the masses under capitalism. History shows class struggle; classical Russian literature carries lessons of oppression and dedication to the revolutionary cause. Study of Marxism-Leninism accompanies and supposedly helps with Russian and mathematics. The youth should emerge with an overwhelming sense of duty. As *Pravda* comments, "It occurs in some families that they drag out, as a reason for studying, the undesirable contention, 'Study is for you, not me; study for your own benefit.' This formula is deeply wrong. It is necessary to convince children otherwise: 'Study because this is necessary for the country, the people. The educated person increases our strength. Study because, when you are grown, you must return a hundredfold what you receive in childhood . . .' "5

The fact that higher education is increasingly the qualification for entry into the upper strata creates problems, and parents resort to all means to open doors for their offspring. It also compels conformity. Entry depends not only on academic considerations but on political acceptability, attested by the Komsomol, or trade-union or party if the candidate has been at work. There are party commissions for the supervision of admissions. Having leaped the hurdle into the university, the student does not seem to have to study very hard. But he must be careful: the security police has representatives at higher institutions and the Komsomol is responsible for discipline. To get his degree, he has to pass courses in dialectical materialism. Ideological problems are severest in social sciences; better students prefer the physical sciences. But it is not easy to escape politics, for in the party's view even mathematics instructors should carry on ideological work.

The Soviet leadership wishes to have rational and creative scientists and engineers who will not bring into question the party's supreme right. Much of the future depends on how far this is possible.

LITERATURE AND THE ARTS

In the creative arts the party faces most acutely the fundamental contradiction between initiative and ideological-political controls. Creativity in every area, from industrial design to theater, is essential for the modern state and for the party's mission of shaping thought and character; yet writers and artists cannot be simply left free to follow their genius. Policy regarding the arts has consequently fluctuated like economic policy; the state of Soviet literature is a good barometer of political pressures.

The revolution was greeted as liberation for the arts, and censorship at first was merely of the kind one finds in Western states in wartime; nothing was to be published attacking the Soviet system. In the enthusiasm for change and experimentation, modernism and futurism flourished; if Lenin did not approve, he did not try to repress artists. Art was practically given over to private enterprise, and the party took the position that various tendencies could contribute to socialism. Artistically, this was the most productive period the Soviet Union has known.

After 1928, Stalin harnessed the arts. All private art groups, organizations and schools were dissolved by official fiat. Publishers were ordered to emphasize socially useful literature, and the authorities began stating explicitly what authors should say. Stalin called writers "engineers of souls" in the five-year plans and invited them to become part of the privileged apparatus of political guidance, with corresponding material and moral rewards. In 1932-34, the Union of Soviet Artists and the Union of Soviet Writers were set up as sole organizations within which artists and writers could function. The obligatory style became "Socialist Realism."

It is not easy to define Socialist Realism. Officially, it is "realist in style, socialist in content." In style, it is pseudofactual, with photographic detail, sober, rather suitable for elementary school textbooks. It permits no art for art's sake. Its socialist content is support of the party and its purposes; under Stalin this degenerated to rather simple-minded propaganda, in the line of boy and girl love tractor. It is anti-individualistic and antisubjective, and strong on positive thinking; it glorifies work, discipline, and self-sacrifice for the state and the party. Its heroes are heroic and its villains despicable. The heroes always win; Man, uplifted by the party, can achieve anything. This has remained the ordinary mode of Soviet writing to this day.

As a result of Stalinist compression, hardly anything of real literary worth, except some wartime pieces, was published in the Soviet Union from 1932 to 1953. Upon Stalin's death, there appeared a rash of critical novels, like Ehrenburg's *The Thaw*, of a sort not seen for nearly a generation. Despite setbacks from time to time, the scene became increasingly varied and interesting through the remaining Khrushchev years. The intellectual community was growing steadily, and its less conformist members could look to expanding support. The scientists patronized modern art and the public flocked to applaud less conformist poets. The party encouraged literary "conservatives," but the liberals managed to gain, and for several years hold, some control of the writers' and artists' organization. Many demanded more integrity and humanity, more opening to the West, and a degree of freedom within the generally accepted framework of socialism and party direction.

The first moves after the ouster of Khrushchev further heartened the liberals; but since the summer of 1965 the collective leadership has worked steadily to restore full party control. Their style has been quite different from that of Khrushchev and more effective. Avoiding personal commitment, they have let hack writers and cultural bureaucrats wage the battle with quiet party backing. A pall of uniformity thickened; more and more movies and books glorified the party line, patriotism, and the military. Even plays of Chekhov were rejected because they might be interpreted as critical of Soviet society. After August, 1968, there were harsher denunciations of Western influence, and remaining liberals were removed from journalistic positions. The redomestication of the arts is suggestive of Stalinist "partyness." Poets like Yevtushenko have been among the freest of writers, but "The white heat of ideological battle demands that our poetic weapon be in good working order and not miss the target. For 'song and verse, these are bomb and banner,' as Maiakovsky wrote."[6]

Party policy is enforced not only by censorship (and sometimes the police) but by the unions, to which artists and authors must belong if they are to be considered professionals eligible for display or publication. Party cells within them are responsible for directing them in the same spirit as party groups guide enterprises toward higher productivity. Party members should carry on political education and teach Marxist-Leninist esthetics to their fellow artists, who should accept ideological guidance as a worker would receive technical instructions.

On admission to the union, an artist or writer is assured of lifelong comfort with moderate exertions and of a high income by Soviet standards if he shows ability. But if the writers are among the least worked and best paid in Soviet society, they need special skills to interest their readers, to draw a credible picture, and to satisfy the party at the same time. It is particularly difficult to portray the party plausibly as it wishes to see itself; yet it is impossible to deal with much in Soviet life without taking the party into account. Suspense comes hard when the triumph of virtue is foreordained; even *Swan Lake* has received a happy ending. Comedy is difficult because there can be no joking at the expense of authority. Crime is usually unacceptable. There should be no disquiet or unsolved problems. There should not even be much depiction of individual feeling; and sex can be used only in Victorian doses. There are supposedly no real conflicts within Soviet society. To find conflicts, Soviet writers may turn to the class struggles of the past or of the "capitalist" world. They particularly dwell on the heroic times of the civil war or the Great Patriotic War, or have glorious security police trap perfidious foreign spies. Or they write nature stories or children's books. In the few plays or novels which treat contemporary Soviet reality, the plot is likely to rest on accident.

It is equally difficult for the party to make the creative artistic intelligence a faithful instrument of party-political purposes. There is always pressure for the staging of popular plays instead of correct ones, for the showing of entertaining, especially foreign, films instead of inspiring ones. For the party to denounce a work is to guarantee its popularity.

SCIENCE

Science is even more necessary than literature and art, but it is also troublesome. Scientists, like writers, are privileged, and most of them are politically passive if not convinced adherents of the regime. But they are aware of science in the Western world and of its achievements, usually superior to their own; they receive foreign journals and may meet Western counterparts in international conventions. They know that scientific theories are confirmed by confrontation of hypotheses and conflict of opinions, and they have ventured to suggest this in Soviet publications. Science is oriented toward change in an increasingly conservative society.

Consequently, a few scientists, particularly those of exceptional talent and relatively secure position, speak out for reform or for new approaches which they perceive as essential for scientific progress or the security of humanity. The nuclear physicist Sakharov has several times expressed deep, sometimes bitter, criticisms of the regime, circulated by the underground press. Some of his colleagues have demanded more freedom or respect for rights; many show at least indifference to official ideology. They also shrug off Socialist-Realist art; sophisticated and well paid, they are the chief patrons of the Soviet Union's small corps of modernist painters and sculptors. The scientists seem to have some confidence in their importance for Soviet progress and strength; they feel their community of interest and are mutually defensive, prepared to fight injustice against any of their colleagues as a threat to all.

The party handles the scientists gently, with rewards and persuasion. They are well paid and honored; rather luxurious accomodations were provided for some at Akademgorodok, in central Siberia, to get them away from Moscow. The institutions on which nearly all scientists depend are party-controlled; and the scientist's career is subject to party scrutiny, not only informally but formally. All scientists are to undergo every three years an examination by a panel including trade-union and party officials along with scientists, testing not only scientific but political qualifications.

Even mathematicians are warned against individualism and urged to work with collective and party spirit for the fatherland and the proletariat, as directed by the party. That a scientist should concern himself only with science is cause for alarm. According to a resolution adopted by the Academy of Sciences in the relatively liberal period, "The international obligation of Soviet scholars is to intensify the criticism of bourgeois ideology . . ."[7] The party group in the scientific institute must concern itself with everything in the collective and the moods and thoughts of the researchers. All scientists should participate in political training and so far as possible publish "philosophy." As *Pravda* assures, the success of engineers, teachers, doctors, scientists, and artists "depends on their mastering the dialectics of analysis and party principles in scientific research and ideological work."[8]

Scientists can often satisfy the formal requirements by making an initial bow, citing Lenin, and getting on with their science. But in some areas and at certain times, ideology has seriously interfered and caused unevenness in Soviet achievements. Mathematics and physics have fared best, the first too abstarct for the ideologues, the second closely associated with military power in the nuclear age. Under Stalin, the theory of relativity was theoretically banned and some principles of quantum mechanics, such as complementarity and uncertainty, were tabu; but physicists used them anyway. Because of secrecy, inferior instrumentation, and its military bent, the Soviet space program has reaped far less scientific data than the American. Soviet oceanography is first-rate, perhaps because of naval implications. Chemistry is backward for reasons not immediately evident.

In medical and biological sciences, the interference of ideology has been more damaging. The virtual murder of Soviet genetics by the pseudoscientist Lysenko is notorious but can hardly be exaggerated. Stalin and Khrushchev were seduced by Lysenko's easy answers for agricultural troubles and by the implication that they could remake Soviet man, and so made official his crude doctrines of acquired heredity. Scientific genetics was simply outlawed by party fiat. Geneticists were driven from their positions or, in some cases, under Stalin, violently purged. Something was saved of Soviet genetics only because research continued under the guise of space science or in radiation laboratories under the patronage of nuclear physicists.

There have been comparable impositions by decree in linguistics and anthropology. Soviet psychology has suffered from the mandatory assumption that there can be no real conflicts. Freudianism is excluded not only by official prudery (which negates sexual psychology in general) but by the official opinion that the personality is not shaped by things like libido and the unconscious but by the state and the party. Orthodox Soviet psychology has been based on the work of Ivan Pavlov, a great scientist who would certainly not approve of his theories being turned into dogma. The conditioned reflex seemed to Stalinists to promise the easy training of the perfect Soviet man.

Soviet medicine is extremely varied in quality, with fine techniques and facilities in some places, poor ones in others. Some Soviet instruments have been borrowed by the West; but the Soviets have contributed practically nothing to the medical revolution of the past generation. Soviet medical researchers are also handicapped by lack of published statistics regarding diseases, causes of death, etc. In the 1960's, some Soviet doctors used leeches to bleed patients and advised mud baths for rickets. The excellence of Soviet medicine is not in its science but in the organization which has produced the world's largest corps of doctors and through which medical care is made readily available.

The shadows of ideology and party direction are deepest in social sciences. The purpose of social science is to advance the endeavors of the party; closely linked with Marxism-Leninism and "scientific socialism," one of its main functions is the unmasking of "bourgeois falsehoods." Treatment of recent or contemporary issues is severely restricted. Soviet philosophers should be warriors against ideological coexistence, although in the Khrushchev era it became possible for Soviet scholars seriously to study Western philosophers and even acknowledge some good points. Political studies not serving the regime are excluded, and the Soviet Union has not followed Eastern European countries in the establishment of political science as an academic subject. Soviet sociologists, who are to be counted in dozens, look into such questions as labor turnover, leisure time utilization, incentives, and vocational plans. Their results are sometimes of considerable interest; but their function is to assist in the management of society.

Soviet science suffers from the vices which plague the economy. Research is overcentralized and overcontrolled; scientists are supposed to plan results in accordance with demands from above. They are even more burdened by bureaucracy and paperwork than American investigators; scholars spend a large part of the time on administrative matters. There is overspecialization, and scientists in one area fail to profit by work in another. Secrecy thus reduces cross-fertilization.

The Soviet Union can get results by massive expenditures, compensating for less productivity per worker by employing larger numbers of workers. Expenditures on research and development are approximately equal to those of the United States. But Soviet science still lags except where the Russians wish to concentrate resources on priority objectives.

RELIGION

The party has difficulties not only with science, the most innovative aspect of culture, but with the most traditional, religion. Religion, like science, poses a challenge to the official Soviet creed and the claim to monopoly of truth about human purpose and destiny. Marxism-Leninism must contain, or provide the basis for seeking, answers to all questions; but religion states that there are divine laws above human laws. The party—not priests, tradition, or scriptures—is to determine right and wrong. Salvation is to be sought through the party, not in relations with any higher powers with the mediation of a church. Religion draws away from the guided mainstream of Soviet life. If churches could be eliminated, there would remain only party-dominated organizations in the Soviet land. Religion has the potential to serve as energizer of movements of non-Russians, especially Catholics and Moslems, toward autonomy or independence. It has also seemed antimodern to the Bolsheviks. Atheism stood for science and industrialization, while religion, as practiced in tsarist Russia, stood for superstitious conservatism, for blessing crops instead of applying fertilizer.

A revolutionary party in Russia in 1917 was inevitably opposed to the Orthodox Church. The Bolsheviks were anathema for the church, while Lenin was more bitterly antireligious than Marx. Consequently, the Bolsheviks on attaining power launched a frontal attack on the former official church. Real estate of the church was nationalized and it was deprived of juridical personality. Many priests and bishops were arrested, some were shot, and there were thousands of clashes with religious peasantry in the first years. There was a lull after the civil war, but forcible attacks were renewed in 1928; a secondary purpose of collectivization was to separate the peasants from the church. Most churches were closed and priests were driven out with the kulaks.

Intense antireligious propaganda continued until the German attack, when religious leaders surprised the Bolsheviks by immediately calling on the people to resist while Stalin remained incommunicado in the Kremlin. By 1943, an informal concordat was worked out, whereby the state fully tolerated the church, which supported the war effort and

Soviet foreign policy. Some twenty thousand churches were reopened and relations at times verged on cordiality. Antireligious propaganda, however, was revived after victory. Khrushchev, in his effort to revitalize ideology, intensified the attack. Atheistic lectures, books, movies and television programs flooded the Soviet media. Taxes on churches were increased, and a majority were closed.

Recent policy has continued in the same direction. The school teaches antireligion, and much propaganda plays on themes of the backwardness of religion, its anti-Soviet nature, and its class significance as a means of exploitation and oppression. The ministers or priests are accused of profiteering and immorality, in many cases of being agents of foreign interests. Religion is a bar to success. Since religious ceremonies were bringing many persons to church for the climactic ceremonies of life, from 1959 there were developed competitive civic-Soviet institutions, especially "marriage palaces." Soviet holidays are magnified to detract from religious ones, most importantly the New Year festival overshadowing Christmas.

Practically nothing is legally permitted except the bare bones of church services. Even this is not assured. The state is owner of all church property, and the lease to the congregation can be terminated. Only a few dozen Orthodox priests are trained yearly; there is only one training center for Moslem mullahs and none for rabbis. Practically no religious publications are permitted; proselytizing is illegal, and it is a crime (except for parents) to give children religious instruction. No one under eighteen may join a church or in theory even enter one, except to be baptized. Occasional reports of children being taken from their parents to prevent the inculcation of religious faith are treated approvingly in the Soviet press. "Religious fanaticism" may be regarded as insanity and grounds for confinement. Believers who refuse to participate in Soviet affairs are subject to imprisonment; they are said to form a large part of the prison population. Large areas of the countryside and many large new cities, even of half a million or more, lack churches or formal ministers of religion. How many of the over 54,000 Orthodox churches of 1913 are left is not divulged, but there may not be more than 10%. What remains of the Orthodox Church has been tamed. Under the official Council for the Affairs of the Orthodox

Church, it is tolerated and financially supported; in return it accepts the state power as decreed by God and supports the government which proposes its extermination. Catholicism in Lithuania has few priests, and there are few Lutheran pastors in Latvia and Estonia. Soviet Judaism is practically without rabbis; of several thousand synagogues in tsarist times, a few dozen remain. The Armenian Church, which is useful as a focus for the diaspora, is domesticated like Russian Orthodoxy, but retains vitality. The weakness of conventional churches seems to spawn the growth of unconventional. Many groups have resorted to informal meeting places, in homes or outdoors, under amateur leaders. Radical and illegal sects, like Seventh Day Adventists, Pentecostals, or schismatic Baptists, seem to have thrived; it is against these that most Soviet ammunition is directed.

The Soviet state cannot replace religion. There is ample testimony to a revival of religious feeling in recent years. Infants presented for baptism are said to be more than half of all births in some palces. Russian and Slavophil stirrings among some of the intellectuals and young people have renewed interest in the ancient faith, with its national as well as spiritual meaning. Under the Old Regime, intellectuals were antireligious not because of intellectual doubt but because religion was a crutch of the state. Now religion has become an alternative for those dissatisfied with the established creed.

FOOTNOTES

1. *Pravda*, May 1, 1970.
2. *ibid*, November 13, 1970.
3. *ibid*, August 22, 1969.
4. *Izvestia*, December 18, 1970.
5. *Pravda*, September 22, 1969.
6. *ibid*, October 21, 1969.
7. George Fischer, *Science and Politics, the New Sociology in the Soviet Union* (Cornell University Press, Ithaca, New York, 1964), p. 4.
8. *Pravda*, July 8, 1969.

CHAPTER 13

Coordination
of the Minorities

Management of diverse peoples is as much of a problem for the party, though in a different way, as management of the economy. The West thinks of the Soviet Union as "Russia," a state centered on Moscow and Leningrad, built by the Russian people, culturally and linguistically a Russian entity. Yet to equate "Soviet" with "Russian" obscures the fact that half the population is non-Russian.* The Russians themselves make a good deal of this basic character of the state—and it is fair to speak of Russians in this context, as the leadership is either Russian or Russianized, Russian-speaking and Russian-thinking. "The Soviet people is not some new nation, not a conglomerate of nations, but an international association of more than a hundred large and small nations

---

*According to the 1970 census, the population (241,720,000) included 129 million Russians, 41 million Ukrainians, 9 million Uzbeks, 9 million Belorussians, 6 million Tatars, 5.3 million Kazakhs, 4.4 million Azerbaidzhanis, 3.6 million Armenians, 3.2 million Georgians, 2.7 million Moldavians (Rumanians), etc. The proportion of Russians is probably overstated, as it is based simply on personal declarations to censustakers.

190

and nationalities, free of social and national antagonisms, from mutual emnity and distrust built up over the ages by the exploiting classes."[1] It is the pride and the mission of the Communist party and Soviet state to unite and thereby protect the peoples.

In the official Soviet view, national friction develops because of the exploitation of weaker nations; this cannot occur under Soviet rule, therefore there can be no friction. But the frequency and emphasis with which Soviet ideologues refer to the problem indicates deep preoccupation. Soviet organs point to the importance of nationalism as a live and present danger, far more critical than demands for freedom or democracy.

Minority discontent has long been troublesome. It worried the tsarist empire, and Lenin correctly saw it as an important revolutionary force. After achieving power, Lenin made extensive concessions to minority feeling, not because he had any sympathy for it but because he appreciated its importance. In the Second World War, non-Russians evinced readiness to collaborate with the invading Germans almost everywhere that they could do so; and Stalin testified to anti-Soviet sentiments by his deportation of the Crimean Tatars and several small Caucasian peoples. After the war, anti-Soviet guerrillas were active for several years in both the Ukraine and Baltic areas.

In the following decades, Soviet authorities have from time to time denounced manifestations of "bourgeois nationalism." In recent years the problem has probably become more severe. In some ways, modernization tends to erode separatist feelings, by increasing travel, migration, the mixing of peoples, and spreading a blanket of uniform mass culture over inherited differences. But minorities also become more aware of what sets them apart, of real or fancied inequities, and of the promises of which they might demand fulfillment.

The essence of the Soviet answer is to stress the ideological imperatives of unity around the Russian-party center and to press for administrative, economic, and cultural amalgamation, while still preserving pretenses of freedom. The chief vehicle of the latter is the federal structure and ostensible sovereignty of the Soviet republics which were joined into the Union after the civil war. Much is made of this sovereignity; "The Union Republic is the highest form of statehood," Soviet authors reiterate.

But it is the most insubstantial. Except for the curious provision of freedom to secede, which would be treasonous to invoke, the constitution leaves practically no rights to the republics. Their territory belongs to the Union, their form of government is laid down by it, their ministries operate under it. Oddly, the two powers most strongly reserved to the federal regime in genuine federalisms, foreign affairs and defense, are nominally shared with the republics. The respective ministries are Union-Republican, and the republics are authorized to conduct diplomatic relations and to maintain armed forces. But no republic is permitted to have diplomatic relations with any country; and there does not seem to exist any republic defense ministry, much less military formations.

"Socialist property in the means of production is the economic basis of this union,"[2] because all important property belongs not to the republic but to the Union, which may permit the republic to administer some of it or may take it away at will. Resources go to the center and are doled out to the republics. Economic planning takes no account of republic boundaries and forwards russification as industrial development of agricultural areas brings in Russian workers and managers. There seems to be a deliberate policy of specialization beyond strictly economic considerations in order to increase interdependence.

The instrument of unity upon which Lenin counted and which remains the most important is the Communist party. Although there are branches of the party corresponding to the minority republics, they do not have any of the nominal sovereignty conceded to the republics. There are only minor concessions to their dignity: they have "central committees" instead of simply "committees" as provincial and lesser party organizations enjoy and they convoke "congresses" instead of "conferences." But they are practically equivalent to provincial organizations and are equally bound to obedience to the Central Committee. Their departments are directly subject to the departments of the Central Committee.

The primary decision-making organization is thus kept fully subject to a single direction, and the party rules the republics not only through the government apparatus but through the party machinery at all levels. The leading figures in the republic are not the chairmen of the council of ministers but the party secretaries. Even this organizational bond is not felt quite sufficient, as key positions in non-Russian republics are reserved for Russians or sometimes Ukrainians. Nationals of White Russia, Ukraine, Armenia, and Georgia are considered reliable enough to largely staff the higher ranks of their respective party apparatuses, but in the Baltic republics and especially in central Asia, Russians occupy strategic positions. A usual arrangement has been that the first secretary, presiding over the bureau of the central committee, is a native for appearances, while the second secretary, in charge of the secretariat and holder of the real power, is a Slav.

Somewhat anomalously, although there are a Ukrainian party, an Uzbek party, etc., there is no Russian party, no Russian central committee, etc. This has historical reasons. The original party was called Russian, and the Ukrainian and other parties were set up as branches of it after the revolution as a concession to national sensitivities. When the Soviet Union was formed, the Russian became the Soviet party. To have kept it as the Russian branch of an all-Soviet party would have been in the logic of federalism, but it would have made the Russian party formally equal to the republic parties. There is no need for a nominally Russian party as a pro forma concession to the Russians, who are aware of their superiority. The All-Union party is in reality a Russian party; at the inner center of power, the Secretariat, there has not been a single non-Russian for nearly a decade.

ANTINATIONAL IDEOLOGY

The political structure which holds the nationalities together can work only thanks to ideological cement. Marxism-Leninism justifies the domination of large and potentially independent lands from a distant and alien capital, excuses their incorporation into the Russian-dominated state, even palliates their onetime conquest by tsarist forces.

Marxism overrides nationalism and thrusts it aside as something bourgeois and backward which has no legitimate place in Soviet society. Generated by class antagonisms, it is useful only to the capitalists;

therefore, so far as it shows itself, it must be a result of Western or hostile class influences and should be banished.[3] Nationalism bespeaks individualism and struggle between peoples; it is denounced as narrow and hateful. It is seen as old-fashioned, exemplified by peasant customs. Minority writers are urged to look to things modern, that is, Soviet, or to the glorious common future, not to their peculiar past.

The valid unity is class unity, and the only acceptable struggle is the class struggle. The premise of Leninism is the superiority of the international proletariat, represented by the united party, to all other forces. Class interest required the Lithuanian working people, for example, to fight anti-Soviet Lithuanian guerrillas after the Second World War as a remnant of the exploiting classes. Hence, patriotism and internationalism can be called equivalent, and they epitomize the Russian-Soviet system. "In Soviet patriotism the national and international are united, since it does not divide nations but binds them into a single brotherly family. The internationalism of Soviet patriots shows itself both in the brotherly unity of the peoples of the USSR and in friendship with the toilers of other lands . . ."[4]

Only Russian nationalism is consonant with Soviet patriotism and proletarian internationalism. Marxist proletarianism also rationalized Russian domination because a majority of industrial workers were and still are of Russian nationality despite industrialization in minority regions, and the superiority of the proletariat over the peasantry was translatable into the superiority of urban Russians over villagers of other nationalities. Everywhere the Russians form a large part of the population of the cities, providing an invaluable reservoir of recruits for the party in minority areas and giving a basis for leadership without overt discrimination on the basis of nationality.

The Marxists are right in contending that nationalism is tinged with irrationality and belongs to a certain period of world history. But it remains strong, and the Russians badly need something to put in its place. A partial answer is simply political advertising and propaganda to convince people that the union is good and that their welfare and safety require belonging to the Soviet community, that they really enjoy the highest freedom, and that the Soviet is the way of the future.

But for a philosophic answer and basic psychological approach, a simplistic political Marxism, better than any obvious alternative, justifies the single party rule for all. The Soviet state seems consequently tied to at least the principal Marxist ideas of the dominance of class over national interests until relations among the Soviet peoples have substantially changed.

ASSIMILATION

It is the Soviet hope ultimately to solve the problem of nationalism by creating a homogeneous Soviet-Russian culture. It was Lenin's basic policy to remove the irritation of coercive russification and to encourage native languages and use them to carry the Bolshevik message to the people, proclaiming cultural autonomy coupled with political conformity. The motto was, "National in form but socialist in content." But Lenin took a narrow view of "national," calling cultural national autonomy "a thoroughly bourgeois and deceitful thought."[5] The "national" form came to mean little more than native language and costumes. Literature in minority languages is as controlled as in Russian, so the productions of various Soviet peoples are virtually indistinguishable. Minority languages are used for political literature, Lenin's works and the like, less a means of national self-expression than of indoctrination of the non-Russian-speaking population. Education in the minority language is a recognized right, but the content of education is fully controlled. Folklore and old songs have been reworked to bring in the party and the Soviet homeland. The most fostered aspect of national culture is folk dancing, of which more is made in the Soviet Union than in any other land. This is not only innocuous but associates national with peasant culture, making it more quaint than serious.

Ostensibly there is no russification, only the development of common patterns. The common pattern is called not Russian but Soviet; the Russian language is held to be useful merely as the lingua franca of the different peoples. "The spread of the Russian language does not at all diminish the role and significance of national languages, but, on the contrary, facilitates their mutual enrichment."[6] But the "enrichment" of minority languages comes to resemble the sovereignty of the republics. More and more Russian terms are introduced into many languages, from "Moldavian"[7] to Central Asian dialects. The attack on the latter has been strongest. First, the Turkic speech of the area was rather artificially divided into several different "languages." Then they were shifted, first from the Arabic to the Latin alphabet and then to the Cyrillic used in Russian. The Russian share of the vocabulary rises; a third of the words in an ordinary newspaper in a Central Asian language are likely to be Russian.

The use of Russian is almost mandatory in administration and all economic matters beyond the strictly local. If one wishes to learn about the world or to be entertained, one can hardly avoid Russian. About nine-tenths of Soviet magazines are published in Russian, and the percentage has long been rising. The number of books printed in Russian in 1967 was eleven times the number in Ukrainian, nearly fifty times the number of Uzbek, the nearest competitors. Publications in many small languages, according to Soviet statistics, have been dropping, presumably indicating a gradual phasing out. Radio Moscow is heard everywhere, rebroadcast by local stations; apparently three quarters or more of radio and television programs in minority republics are in the Russian language. Cinema is entirely Russian.

Russian was made obligatory in all schools in 1938, and it seems to be the language of instruction in a steadily growing proportion of the schools of the country. About three quarters of schoolbooks are in the Russian language. Parents are supposed to have free choice to send children to a Russian-language or minority-language school, but the former is probably better and is almost a necessity if children are to go on to higher education, which is largely in Russian. It may also help the political standing of a parent of minority nationality to give this token of loyalty.

Russification is forwarded by the mixing of peoples. Many hundreds of thousands have gone, coerced or voluntarily, to Siberia, Central Asia, and elsewhere around the fringes; as a result, almost everywhere, at least in cities, there is a substantial Russian population to support the regime. Graduates of higher educational institutions, who have to take assigned jobs for two years, are sent away from their republic. Army draftees ordinarily serve away from native republics and are encouraged to remain after their term is finished. Peasants are sometimes given free transportation and bonuses for moving to distant regions. Professional workers are very often employed outside native areas, Baltic technicians in Russia or Central Asia, Russian scientists in the Ukraine and vice versa. One can assume, from the extent of official concern, that political motives are mixed with economic.

That assimilation has had success cannot be doubted. Many small nationalities have been absorbed into the Russian, and some larger ones are under pressure. Not much Ukrainian, for example, is to be heard on the streets of Kiev. In another sense, assimilation is successful in that it has divided the minorities and deprived them of leadership, and persons of talent are largely drawn into the service of the Soviet system. Non-Russians may become superpatriots for the Soviet Union and prominent spokesmen of "proletarian internationalism." Some, like Stalin, have been ruthless in the suppression of minority nationalism. At the 1971 Party Congress, leaders of all major minority nationalities made a point of decrying manifestations of nationalism by their own people, even calling for more "merging" of peoples and cultures.

But there is strong resistance to what would seem overwhelming pressures. In the period 1959-1970 not enough persons were converted to the Russian nationality to compensate for the lower birthrate of the Russians; the percentage of the population calling themselves Russians dropped from 55 to 53.5. And it is apparent that learning Russian does not assure conformity. Only 17.7% of the Jews were recorded as Yiddish-speaking by the last census, yet many young people are demonstrative of their Jewishness. Many tens of thousands brave heavy penalties and pay dearly to apply for emigration visas. Contrariwise, despite Marxist-Leninist ideology, anti-Semitism smolders below the surface and is reflected in sundry discriminations.

If the superficial assimilation of the Jews into Soviet life does not preclude frictions, the same is true of more compact and numerous and less fully russified groups. From time to time the Soviet press complains of efforts to impose the national language (as the minorities see it, to check russification), overemphasis on tradition, or of opposition to exchange of cadres (resentment against the influx of Russians in superior positions). *Pravda* warns of disguised nationalism: "Localism may look like an endeavor to strive for the flourishing of one's own republic, territory, or province . . . underestimation of contacts with fraternal people may be presented as a wish to make the most of one's own possibilities . . ."[8] To combat such tendencies, there are occasional housecleanings in the leaderships of insufficiently vigilant party apparatuses in non-Russian republics, and in nearly all of them there have been repressions.

Those who present by far the severest problem for the Soviet leadership are the underdeveloped nations within the Soviet Union, the Central Asians, peoples markedly different from the Russians by language, culture, religion, and race. There was little integration of the Central Asian provinces and protectorates under the tsars, and the Bolshevik reconquest of the area, carried out with the assistance of Russian colonists, was difficult and bloody. Russification and Sovietization have not been very effective. Collectivization was nominally imposed long ago, but the new kolkhoz is a renamed kin-group. Islam remains strong and has apparently seen a recent upsurge.

The new factories are largely an alien import, like modern establishments built by foreign capital in less developed lands of the non-Soviet world. Productivity remains low. Per capita income in the four Asian republics, Turkmenistan, Kirghizistan, Uzbekistan and Tadzhikistan, averages not much more than half that of the Soviet Union, and that of the indigenous people must be substantially less if account is taken of the higher income of the Russian sector of the population. The gap has been widening in recent years, partly because of birthrates over twice as high among Asiatics as Russians.

One can believe that the Soviet leadership would like to have all treated fairly and to see all equally contented beneath their aegis. In some ways non-Russians may have been favored; the standard of living in some outlying areas, as Georgia, the Ukraine, Latvia, and Estonia is apparently as high as in Moscow. What matters, however, is not the justice or injustice that an outsider might weigh, but the perception of the peoples themselves. Non-Russians may feel psychologically, if not materially disadvantaged; they inevitably chafe under orders from distant and alien decision makers. What Russians are likely to see as simply failures of the regime, minorities can view as exploitation and oppression. Russians may believe it necessary to accept the Soviet system and its imperfections because this is necessary for the integrity of the state. Non-Russians, however, are required to accept russification as well as bolshevization. If the system is in some ways severe with Russians, it is likely to deal more severely with those whose basic loyalty is more questionable. Even though the leadership may desire justice, Russians look down on many non-Russians, for whom they have sundry deprecatory nicknames; Central Asians, for instance, are regarded as dirty. The designation of nationality in passports facilitates informal discrimination. In the innumerable opportunities for the abuse of power, the politically weaker minorities are vulnerable.

Modernization and education raise sensitivities. It was easier for the Bolsheviks to rule in the first years because the non-Russian upper classes were wiped out. Now a new educated elite has been created. Most of these see the way to advancement in collaboration with the system, but some provide potential leadership of disaffection. The economic lag of some areas, especially Central Asia, must be increasingly obvious. As people rise above subsistence levels, political demands become more insistent and more threatening. But the Soviet state has no new answer, and the problem weighs heavily over it.

FOOTNOTES

1. *Pravda*, November 26, 1968.

2. *ibid*, November 26, 1968.

3. Nationalism abroad is considered good so far as it weakens and divides anti-Soviet forces.

4. *Pravda*, November 26, 1968.

5. Quoted by *Sovety deputatov trudiashchikhsia*, no. 1, January, 1969, p. 1.

6. *Dialektika stroitel'stva kommunizma* (Izd. Mysl, Moscow, 1968), p. 243.

7. Romanians living in Bessarabia are treated as a separate nationality, sufferers in the past from Romanian imperialism.

8. *Pravda*, January 24, 1969.

CONCLUSION

The Aging Revolution

A revolution that destroys the basis of the social order, like the Russian Revolution, is a time of great excitement, of stark fears for the loss of old values, and of indefinite hopes that an infinitely better world can be made. It is a time of new aspirations and rethinking of problems, of revitalization and reintegration of society around new purpose. New men, energetic and dedicated, grasped control of the Russian state in 1917, as outworn structures and a mass of corrupt and corrupting privileges were swept away. The new social order, coupled with the reinforced sense of Russian destiny, gave large numbers of persons a profound sense of importance and purpose. The Bolsheviks, feeling that they had something to live and die for, set about realizing the potentials of Russia. It was a bright new dawning after a long darkness of disappointments and defeats. Victory in the civil war, in which the Bolsheviks felt they had turned back the united forces of world capitalism, deepened convictions of glorious destiny.

But a revolution must be young to be revolutionary. The euphoric fever could not last indefinitely, and it receded as the men who made the revolution left the scene. The inauguration of the five-year plans, a great novelty at the time, helped rejuvenate the revolution; but the Soviet system was becoming decadent by the beginning of the Second

World War. This was evident from the unbelievably poor showing of the Red Army against Finland, the self-deception of the top leadership and its deafness to all warnings, the sluggishness with which the government reacted to the German invasion, and the incapacity of the military forces in the first weeks. But Nazi brutality and the threat to Russian national existence restored morale. Capable generals replaced intriguers and bootlickers. The common purpose of people and government was revived. National character was reshaped in the crucible of a sacred and glorious struggle, the importance of which is shown by the large role it is given in the literature and entertainment media to this day. Victory vindicated and stiffened the Soviet structure and ideology, and the resultant elan showed itself in the high growth rates of the first postwar decade.

The searing and inspiring experiences, from the storming of the winter palace to the capture of Berlin, are now history to a majority of the Soviet population, a history not only distant in time but of a different world. Although many Soviet institutions and the language and style of politics have superficially remained much as they were decades ago, the Soviet Union is materially another country from that of the latter 1920's, when Stalin was moving toward dictatorial power. It was then a peasant land, four-fifths rural, largely illiterate and with only a handful of well educated persons. Now it is industrialized, with a population three-fifths urbanized, with high literacy, and with the world's largest number of highly trained professionals. Poverty and the struggle to get enough to eat have given way to moderate affluence and style-consciousness. Revolutions, so far as our experience tells us, are made only in premodern countries; the concern of the Soviet people has shifted from the reordering of society to the enjoyment of the good life. The generation gap between the elders tempered by civil conflict, famine, purges, and war and the faddish Soviet youth is probably deeper than any American equivalent. Many aspects of material progress also tend to erode authority. Modern communications and education increase people's awareness of themselves and of the affinities and rights promised them. The educated are less easily satisfied with dogmatic simplifications, and often look down on political leaders whose knowledge is inferior to their own. The advanced industrial economy outgrows crude political controls and requires many persons of special skills, whom political leaders must take into account. It becomes more difficult to combine technical expertise with party skill and dedication. Force and coercion become less effective means of government; the regime must rely more on incentives, which raise the standing of the recipients. The very fact that people are urbanized makes them harder to govern than landbound and immobile peasants. The city permits the individual to lose himself in anonymous masses; it gives choice of occupations and associations. The metropolis, a meeting place of ideas, has always been a breeding ground of heterodoxy, if not opposition. With increasing mobility people can become politically more active. The growth of international trade and contacts undermines opinion controls. The more complex society raises innumerable questions hard to decide by political means.

Controls become more difficult in many ways. At least a few people can listen to foreign broadcasts; some can put together their own transmitters. When everyone has a telephone, the KGB cannot eavesdrop on a considerable fraction. The Soviets have a new problem in controlling the use of photocopiers. Education generates discontent of minority nationalities; most of the Ukrainian dissidents who have come to the attention of the West, for example, are intellectuals or students. Educated or semieducated young people in the major cities are bored with ideology and official art and are curious about the outside world and eager to travel. The intelligentsia becomes too numerous to keep under any sort of surveillance. Censorship becomes a problem with larger numbers of more technical publications. The teaching of foreign languages opens up subversive influences. Many thousand Soviet citizens have close contacts with foreigners, and many thousand foreigners are brought into the Soviet Union for business needs. Tourism, although informal contacts are minimized, entails some opening, while it means a little leak in the foreign trade monopoly and nourishes a small class of independent traders ("speculators").

The ideology of revolution has less appeal for the better educated younger generation and less application to modern society. As a Soviet writer puts it, "present-day youth has not gone through the vital school of revolutionary class struggle, in which the convictions and the class awareness of the older generation were formed."[1] The emotions which propelled the Leninists are far away. The ideals of equality and the utopia to be found once the workers took power from the capitalists are empty slogans. Revolutionary promises, whether realized or failed, have lost their interest. The party tries to keep ideology alive by an immense effort of indoctrination, the magnitude of which testifies to its difficulty, as though seeking to replace elemental appeal by ceaseless incantation. The Soviet state has ceased to be a revolutionary way and has become an established order, valuing stability much more than change. It is probably harder for Soviet leaders to believe in their own doctrines, and their children turn away from political commitment.

Soviet society has become correspondingly more traditional, less Communist and more Russian. It has rediscovered the past on a large scale. Soviet writers speak of a general revival of old customs; it is even urged that Soviet intellectuals steep themselves in Russia's historical past, not the "nihilism" of the 1920's.[2] Collecting icons, peasant art, and antiques is very fashionable. Every town is to have its museum of local, especially military, history. Russians flock to view old churches and expensively restored architectural monuments. The worker entering a factory receives a booklet recounting its history. Collective farms write up chronicles of their history, build monuments to heroes who fell in the revolution and the wars, and study regional history. They revive traditional celebrations and develop new ones to commemorate the induction of new members, marriages, births, the sendoff of recruits to the army, the first furrow of spring, and the completion of the harvest.[3] Numerous books have been published about the new Soviet ceremonies, not only the Soviet versions of the traditional rites of marriage and death but new ones such as receiving a passport or entering a factory work force. No country is fonder of distinctions and awards.

As the revolution has grown old, it has turned into a status quo. Stalin was the last revolutionary; Khrushchev sought to go back to Leninism, and his grand schemes amounted to little more than tinkering with basic policies, as in the amalgamation of the collective farms. When he tampered with party structure, and divided it into agricultural and industrial sectors, the apparatus rose against him. Changes since

Khrushchev have been mostly reversions to Stalinism. Those in positions of authority increasingly form a new elite, or a new ruling class as it has been termed—the new owners of the state. These political specialists and managers are truly, as Djilas stressed, a new class in the Marxian sense, controlling the means of production as well as the means of force. The successors of those who made the revolution in the name of the proletariat have become not a new bourgeoisie but a service nobility, with position dependent not on possession but on political relations and loyalty to their superiors. Party work is the highest of professions. Men of medium and higher levels are practically owners of their status; even if they get into trouble, they are normally simply removed to an equivalent post.

Secrecy reinforces status; those on the inside have access to knowledge corresponding to their responsibilities. Status implies material privileges; the times when high Bolsheviks lived ascetically and received a worker's pay are long past. Rewards are less in income than in perquisites. A Komsomol chief in a small republic may make only about four times as much as an ordinary worker, so that he can hardly afford a car; but he is furnished a chauffeured limousine. The state or party provides apartments, dachas, servants, travel, and expense accounts. A form of wealth is the prerogative of buying in special shops, where foreign wares or off-season fruits and vegetables are sold at modest prices, or in foreign currency shops. The elect hunt in reservations closed to ordinary people and sun themselves on private beaches.

Unlike Lenin, Soviet leaders who call on the people to put in an extra day's work for a "Communist Saturday" do not deign to turn out to lay a symbolic brick. It is held important to "maintain the dignity of a Soviet functionary." Distance between teacher and students should be maintained. When a teacher told his pupils, "You should prepare your lesson carefully. I also prepare every day, because I am no god and can't know everything," he was chided for reducing the magisterial authority.[4] Status is everywhere in the "classless" society. The young people of today need more work, less book learning, *Izvestia* complains.[5] Ordinary farm workers take off their hats to the brigade leader, *Pravda* reports.[6] The horror of an educated family that the son should marry a slightly less educated girl was recently subject of a successful drama in Moscow.[7]

The fading of idealism and the establishment of new privileges entail creeping corruption. Countless persons are in a position to be helpful to others by stretching or violating rules, or simply by exercising options, and they are more likely to expect material compensation as the system loses dynamism and officials gain more security. It is apparently common if not customary to require extra payment for routine services, such as entering a freight shipment, issuing a bill of health, or assigning living space. Or a bank, before finalizing a building loan, demands the assignment of several future apartments to its own staff. Such innocuous but important cheating as getting false character references for entry to higher education arouses little indignation, as reported in the press, and calls for no punishment.

There is evidently much sympathy and understanding for well-placed malefactors and incompetents, although in the older Bolshevik ethic the common standards were supposed to apply more strictly to them than to ordinary people. Traffic police look the other way when party men commit violations. For more serious offenses, it is evidently up to the party organization to decide whether a transgressor should be tried in court or subjected to party discipline only. When the manager of a truck depot loaned some trucks to an enterprise in return for cash, he was given a "severe reprimand."[8] About the same time, a bookkeeper who assigned an apartment for a bribe was sentenced to four years.[9] Both cases were reported as correct procedure. In another case, a party man who privately sold goods produced in his factory was not even removed from the buro of his party organization.[10] A fairly well-placed poacher seems to be able to carry on a large-scale business with practical impunity.[11] The real wealth, however, is political position, so the real and invisible corruption is the improper securing or dealing in status.

The state has inevitably lost effectiveness as it has lost drive and become ingrown and more self-seeking. The immense administrative machinery built up to carry out the central will develops its own ways, interests, and interrelations. As revolutionary purposes become irrelevant, power-holders at all levels use power for their own, as well as governmental purposes. The leadership loses the ability to move the bureaucratic and rule-bound apparatus, and the apparatus to move the people; a legally unlimited government undertakes no substantial reforms.

How far this has proceeded in the Soviet Union one can only guess. But it is clear that orders do not count as they once did. A Ukrainian county party committee in 1969 took up the work of a chemical factory seven times, passed appropriate resolutions, and changed nothing.[12] Novosibirsk University prepared 150 teachers for rural schools, but only eight showed up for work.[13] There have been many complaints in the Soviet press against "pirates" on the air, breaking the official monopoly of broadcasting, even hampering communications at Moscow's main airport. In some places in Siberia almost all the fur trade is in the hands of illegal dealers; the only remedy suggested was to raise state prices.[14] The unregulated and more or less illegal sector of the economy may be growing more rapidly than the controlled sectors; street selling is reported to be ever more massive in Baku.[15] Despite emphasis on preventive medicine, there was an epidemic of cholera in southern Russia in 1970, a disease usually associated with underdeveloped countries. The Soviet state is no more successful than Western ones in battling alcoholism. Central coordination may fail; in one case, there were severe losses because the Ministry of Agricultural Construction and the Ministry of Industrial Construction could not agree on procedures, and no solution was envisaged.[16] There has been much lyrical propaganda about the development of Western Siberia, the great Soviet storehouse of raw materials, but population growth there was only 8% from 1959 to 1970, against 16% for the country as a whole. The cultivated area of the largest Siberian district, Yakutia, decreased from 137,700 hectares in the early 1950's to 62,000 in 1969.[17] The party seems to have given up, as the 1971-75 plan turned back to developing the established centers.

Sovietization has failed to advance in Central Asia, and perhaps has even been reversed. East Europe has become increasingly difficult to manage, or the means of managing it have weakened. In 1968, it became necessary to send an army into Czechoslovakia, previously a faithful satellite under merely party controls, to keep it obedient. Some liberalization in the bloc was tolerated under Khrushchev, sometimes even pushed by Moscow for the sake of modernization; now it seems to be tolerated because of the difficulty of repressing it.

The economy responds sluggishly to the stimulants perpetually applied, and exhortation and concentration of resources on productivity bring minimal results. The Soviet share of world trade (including exchanges with the bloc) decreased from 4.3% in 1960 to 4.0% in 1969, and the Soviet share of world industrial production at best remained stable during that period. There is no longer talk of quickly overtaking the United States but a likelihood of being surpassed by Japan. It is anomalous that a modern industrial power should have a large number of shops in which its currency is not acceptable and in which choice Soviet goods are four, even five times cheaper than in open stores. Despite thousands of articles, control commissions, tinkering with planning devices, and even substantial investment, agricultural output has been painfully sluggish since 1958. Despite larger investments, a growth of only 20-22% is foreseen for 1971-1975. The ratio of output to capital has declined over almost all of Soviet history, whereas elsewhere it has regularly risen because improved technology makes capital more productive.[18] In the 1960's the Soviet Union reverted to the large-scale importation of Western factories and technicians to run them, as in the 1930's, despite the political cost. Not only leading industrial powers are called upon to help; the Finns built a hotel in Tallinn; the Yugoslavs give technical assistance on cattle-feeding equipment.

The police seems less zealous in enforcing the dictates of the rulers, following, albeit at a distance, in the footsteps of the tsarist police. This, together with the decline of conviction on the part of the governors and of ideological acceptance by the governed of their right to rule, has made it possible for increasing numbers of persons to challenge the regime. In the 1930's, the government could squeeze the church practically out of organized existence. New weapons have been added to the legal arsenal, and the official position opposing religion is unchanged, but growing numbers ignore or defy the will of the party. Jews protest, sometimes even taunt the police, and demand to emigrate. Public demonstrations against official policies have been on a small scale, but such lapses would have been inconceivable in Stalin's time and unthinkable in Khrushchev's.

The old counterrevolutionary opposition has been forgotten, and within Soviet society there has arisen a new opposition against the new elite. The community of dissident writers, scientists, and other intellectuals is very small, but it is gifted, mutually protective, and often courageous; it may become fashionable, as it was in tsarist times. Its chief achievement is a substantial underground literature. From the latter 1950's there has been a swelling volume of illegal publications by "Samizdat" ("Self-Publisher"), which has emerged particularly since the party began withdrawing much of the limited freedom to which the intelligentsia became accustomed under Khrushchev. It is sometimes handwritten but mostly typewritten privately or in offices; this can perhaps be done at government expense, so a book by Samizdat is not necessarily extremely expensive. Most of the material seems to be poems or novels, some of them translated; countless satirical songs also defy censorship. There are also critical statements which may receive much wider publicity as they come into the hands of Western broadcasters. Since April, 1968, there has circulated every two months a "Chronicle of Current Events," devoted mainly to the defense of rights of Soviet citizens. A single issue has some thirty pages, and its coverage shows access to police sources.

Active oppositionists are not numerous and apparently almost confined to Moscow and Leningrad, strong only in the widespread though mostly passive support of many of the educated elite. They are also ideologically weak. The protesters usually accept the premises of the regime and use its vocabulary; they have no real alternative program and no unifying philosophy. Most do not seem to wish to overthrow the regime but merely to secure the implementation of proclaimed rights; they see their mission in terms of purifying the party and getting back to the true ideals of Marxism-Leninism, without realizing that these do not provide a firm basis for political freedom. A few take a neo-revolutionary or Maoist position, rejecting the Soviet system as a reversion to capitalism. Some look to Western models and wish to open up and liberalize the system to make Soviet democracy a reality, warning that reforms are essential to prevent the Soviet Union from falling behind in competition with the West. Others wish to mingle Marxism-Leninism with Russian nationalism or nostalgic Pan-Slavism, calling for a return to popular roots, perhaps with religious overtones. There are also neo-Stalinists, who have nothing in common with the liberal intellectuals except opposition to the establishment. Divided and uncertain, the oppositionists can only suggest reform, not radical remaking of the system. Nonetheless, the feeble intellectual opposition brings the basis of the Soviet regime into question and casts doubt upon its future.

OUTLOOK

For the present, the Soviet system seems firm and stable. It is strong in ways which are real although somewhat different from those usually emphasized by its apologists. The Soviet Union has a coherent social order which elevates public purpose and gives economic and psychological security. The Soviet state offers the common man a role, plays up to him at least verbally, tries to give him a feeling that what he has to do has some superior value, and insists that his is an equalitarian society. Everyone belongs to a collective, from the school class to the workers' group or social organization. Thanks to the sense of belonging and of playing a part in a movement of deep significance, many strongly favor the system regardless of ideology.

From birth to death, the Soviet citizen has to make few independent choices; after having picked his professional specialization his course is largely fixed. Soviet émigrés find it oppressive to have to decide countless matters such as where they will live and when they will take vacations. The state also relieves its citizens of moral and philosophical uncertainty. There are no problems of values to perplex Soviet man, no reason to stand in awe of the mysterious universe or to try in vain to make an older ethics fit a distraught modernity. The all-knowing party gives answers to all fundamental questions, answers which may be more satisfying for many than the confusion of Western society. The party's interpretation of universal purpose and the direction of history is agreeable for Soviet people, in its updated version of the old Russian vision of universal order and salvation. It is self-congratulatory, an always comfortable approach.

The Soviet system represents, at least outwardly, direction and order in a world that often seems directionless and disorderly. Its patriotism is uncomplicated, of unqualified right and duty. Its art is simple and its values uncomplicated. Soviet citizens are shielded from what they are taught to regard as the depravity and decadence of the West—amorality and class, social, and racial conflict, and petty squabbling among nations. If capitalism is unstable, the "socialist" system offers, at least in theory, harmony and stability. Boys happily "grow up in awareness of our rightness on earth."[19] People are given to understand that they are happy; and if they are not, they must be perverse, whereas in the West they are encouraged always to demand more. Anyone who compares the didactic severity of Soviet cinema and television with the diet of violence, frivolity, and sex of Western productions must question whether the former may not have survival value in a competitive world. Soviet literature and the press are uplifting, glorifying good deeds, heroism, and self-sacrifice.

More important than the fact that the Soviet system carries conviction for most of the people is the fact that it suits the elite very well; a small minority can rule comfortably a discontented majority if the rulers only remain united and determined. For this the Soviet structure of successively narrower and more privileged circles is admirably fashioned; all parts share an interest in the maintenance of the apparatus. To rise, people must invest in a training which fits them only for the party career, and the farther people rise in various sectors, the more their interests converge.

The elite has a vested interest in the power of the party, which is not only an organization but a moral value. It is the unifier of the tremendous realm, and this is the basic justification for everything else which comprises the Soviet way, planned economy, police controls, sham elections and elected bodies, censorship, official creed, and monopoly of organization. There is no telling how else the hundred-odd nationalities on a sixth of the earth's surface could be held together. The party does all in its power, furthermore, to exclude any alternative by the destruction of all other political groups and tendencies; any unofficial or spontaneous political activity is a danger to the system, no matter how fully its goals coincide with those proclaimed for the revolution. The Soviet Union remains totalitarian in that there is no independent organization. The alternative to party rule is anarchy, the ultimate evil. Even if one should hate the party, one can hardly contemplate its overthrow, much as the Germans kept obedient to Hitler long after they knew the war was lost because he had removed all other institutions of leadership. Likewise, victims of the purges would uphold to the end their loyalty to the party which was persecuting them. The safety of the state has always been the supreme law. Once it required, or seemed to require, the burghers' prostrating themselves before the despot of Muscovy; now it requires or seems to require the apparatus of the Soviet state. To be against the party is to oppose the entire order of society.

For the longer term, however, the Soviet Union lacks an essential of the stable political system, an orderly means of change of leadership. A system whereby men select their own colleagues and successors and are removed only by death or Byzantine intrigue can hardly fail to imply decadence. There has, indeed, been a clear progression in Soviet leadership, as each succession of a generation has meant a change of quality, a step away from revolutionary beginnings. If Lenin was a revolutionary intellectual, Stalin was a machine politician. Lenin was a thinker and political analyst; Stalin was relatively crude and afraid of the competition of more sophisticated Marxists. Still, Stalin earned the respect of the world; and his writings, at least up to the time of his absolutism, were often fairly well reasoned and quotable. Khrushchev was a less impressive leader with few pretensions to ideological authority. The present leaders seem to lack even Khrushchev's peasant flair and limited idealism, although they may be more methodical and careful.

If the party does not advance the most dynamic men to the top, this accords with timeless political principles. Those on top have chosen their own lieutenants; and the leader who has more position than security does not want next to him persons who may threaten his standing. Lenin surrounded himself with men willing to defer entirely to him; there was no room for outstanding minds at his side, although he permitted some intellectual independence to those, like Bukharin, whom he trusted. Stalin, a dictator without dictatorial office or legitimacy, was insanely suspicious of anyone who seemed to offer a possible alternative to his leadership. Some capable men, like Malenkov, Molotov, and Khrushchev, managed to survive around Stalin only by entirely submerging their own personalities. Khrushchev in turn sought to get rid of the more self-assertive of his associates, and one can assume that he endeavored to fill the top echelon with people whom he saw as innocuous.

The aging of the revolution has entailed the aging of the leadership. Lenin, at forty-seven, was the oldest important member of the first Soviet government; the average age of the Politburo in 1917 was thirty-six. Since then it has tended irregularly upwards, until in 1971 it was sixty-one. For four years, there has not been one demotion, retirement, or addition to the little group composed of Central Committee Secretaries and full and candidate members of the Politburo.

Senescence thus looms for the oligarchic leadership, which seems to lack capacity for renewal of personnel or institutional change. The present system must soon require revitalization and overhaul. A new dictatorship might rejuvenate and enliven to some extent, and this cannot be viewed as unlikely. The Soviet system contains impediments to dictatorship but may require it; it has usually, of course, had a dictator to cap the political edifice. But a true revitalization can be brought about only by another great trauma, like war or another revolution.

In summary, the Soviet Union suffers from the ancient vices of uncontrolled power. It has been invigorated by upheavals and ordeals and it has drawn inspiration from its revolutionary ideology. But it has shown no ability to solve the problems of decadence and corruption of absolutism, and these grow as the purer and healthier inspiration recedes and the system becomes ingrown and self-seeking.

It is likely to be difficult to find a solution. Political power hardly checks itself, and there is very little external pressure to reform. The tsarist empire was driven to political improvement from time to time by military defeat, but there is no physical threat to Soviet security. The tsarist regime was bombarded with demands and proposals for political change; such public discussion is outlawed in the Soviet Union. Nor are economic shortcomings likely to generate much pressure for change as long as the party holds firmly to power; many an authoritarian regime has comfortably dominated impoverished populations for long periods.

Change is probably also impeded by well based fears that it is dangerous, that any crack in the structure of authority could lead to grave fissures. Economic relaxation might lead to political relaxation. Permitting a contest in some elections could raise demands for freedom of political agitation and real elections everywhere. Giving any reality to representative institutions would provide a forum and focus for discontents and divisions now hidden. In tsarist times, the feeble and unrepresentative Duma contributed to the growth of nationality feelings; in the Supreme Soviet, minority deputies would only have to ask for the realization of the fulsome promises of independence and autonomy. It is difficult to imagine what would happen in a democratic Russia, with its tensions and authoritarian mentality. Few seem to try to imagine, but repeat the common phrase, "The people need a leader."

Concessions to the national minorities would be especially perilous. Given a modicum of autonomy, the republics might become effective pressure groups clamoring for more autonomy. Anything yielded to one republic would become harder to deny to others. One of the first demands would be relief from censorship and permission for national self-expression. But literary gatherings easily become political manifestations, and taking off the lid would permit national consciousness to boil over. To devolve management of the economy would be to give a firmer basis for demands for autonomy. Without a unified system of control, planned economies strongly tend toward autarky; "National communisms" would develop, as they threatened to do in the relaxation of the 1920's. The whole order would be called into question. Relaxation of control of the satellites would be similarly risky, as concessions to one would raise demands of others, and the Ukrainians would ask why they should not have democratic communism if this were permitted the Czechs; it was hence necessary to crush Dubček and the Czech liberalization movement in 1968.

Many persons long thought that the Bolshevik experiment must fail because it was excessively radical and unconventional. This was an error. Its successes came primarily because it could make new beginnings; if it is incompetent and unsuccessful, this is rather because it is basically conservative and too much like authoritarian systems of the past. The question now is whether this modernized, politically immobile system with its revolutionary ideology can find ways to regularize and make permanent something like the present self-choice of leadership, or whether it will somehow find the way to substantial reshaping of the edifice of authority. This would imply division and limitation of power, but the central principle of the Soviet state is the concentration and fullness of power.

FOOTNOTES

1. *Kommunist,* no. 8, August 1970, p. 29.
2. *Nash sovremmenik,* January, 1970. *ABSEES,* July, 1970. p. 91; *Molodaia gvardiia,* July, 1970. *ABSEES,* January, 1971, p. 3.
3. *Selskaia zhizn,* October 22, 1969.
4. *Sovetskaia Estoniia,* October 28, 1970.
5. *Izvestia,* December 18, 1970.
6. *Pravda,* May 25, 1970.
7. *Unequal Marriage,* by V. Konstantinov and B. Ratser.
8. *Pravda,* August 11, 1969. Current Digest, vol. 21, no. 32.
9. *ibid,* August 13, 1969. *ibid,* vol. 21, no. 33.
10. *ibid,* January 20, 1970.
11. *ibid,* August 14, 1969.
12. *Partinaia zhizn,* no. 22, November, 1970.
13. *Sovestkaia Rossiia,* November 14, 1970.
14. *ibid,* January 31, 1971.
15. *Bakinskii rabochii,* February 18, 1971.
16. *Pravda,* April 29, 1970.
17. *Selskaia zhizn,* December 25, 1969.
18. Cohn *The Development of the Soviet Economy* ed. G. Treml (Praeger, New York, 1969), p. 36.
19. *Pravda,* May 1, 1971.

INDEX

217